# WHAT PEOPLE ARE SAYING ABOUT
## *SPIRITUAL LIFE HACKS*

"Len hits upon issues in this book that everyone can identify with...exhaustion, fear, complacency, doubt, and more. His use of humor and wise, biblical insights will keep readers coming back for more, page after page. This book is a fun read that will help everyone who reads it grow spiritually."

**Stephen Arterburn,**
Bestselling author, founder of *New Life Live* and *Women of Faith*, teaching pastor, and, most importantly, dad and husband

"Len Woods is a master at offering practical suggestions, specific insights, and helpful applications. *Spiritual Life Hacks* challenged me to find realistic ways to refocus my day and to cling to God and His truth. I'm incredibly grateful for Len's pastoral heart, and I pray this book will be an encouragement to others."

**Christopher D. Hudson,**
General editor of the *NIV Bible for Men*

"Len Woods makes my life better. *Spiritual Life Hacks* is fresh, interesting, and filled with truth. Best of all, it's not just a long list of burdensome instructions but a warm collection of reminders that spiritual growth is a normal, joyful part of a relationship with Christ. This one is easily recommended."

**Mike Nappa,**
Bestselling and award-winning author

"Len Woods has a gift. It's the ability to simplify how we can act (or react!) to the way things stack up. Much like MacGyver constructs creative solutions, Len ties ordinary words together that yield extraordinary solutions to our stressful situations. Are you ready to use the spiritual life hacks he's forged for you to find uncommon solutions for common challenges? I am."

**Susan B. Mead,**
Award-winning author of *Dance with Jesus* and *Don't Go Through Life Naked*

# Spiritual Life Hacks

## LEN WOODS

**HARVEST HOUSE PUBLISHERS**
EUGENE, OREGON

Cover design by Bryce Williamson

Cover photos © bsd555, LokFung, Kayocci, Yevhenii Dubinko, pseudodaemon, Maljuk / Getty Images

Published in association with The Steve Laube Agency, LLC, 24 West Camelback Road, A 635, Phoenix, Arizona 85013

**Spiritual Life Hacks**
Copyright © 2019 by Len Woods
Published by Harvest House Publishers
Eugene, Oregon 97408
www.harvesthousepublishers.com

ISBN 978-0-7369-7850-7 (pbk)
ISBN 978-0-7369-7851-4 (eBook)

Library of Congress Cataloging-in-Publication Data

Names: Woods, Len, author.
Title: Spiritual life hacks / Len Woods.
Description: Eugene : Harvest House Publishers, 2019. | Includes
   bibliographical references.
Identifiers: LCCN 2019000516 (print) | LCCN 2019009128 (ebook) | ISBN
   9780736978514 (ebook) | ISBN 9780736978507 (pbk.)
Subjects: LCSH: Christian life—Miscellanea. | Bible—Miscellanea.
Classification: LCC BV4501.3 (ebook) | LCC BV4501.3 .W659 2019 (print) | DDC
   248.4--dc23
LC record available at https://lccn.loc.gov/2019000516

**Printed in the United States of America**

19 20 21 22 23 24 25 26 27 / VP-SK / 10 9 8 7 6 5 4 3 2 1

"I WANT TO HELP YOU TO GROW AS BEAUTIFUL AS GOD MEANT
YOU TO BE WHEN HE THOUGHT OF YOU FIRST."

*THE MARQUIS OF LOSSIE*, GEORGE MACDONALD

*To Cindi…*

*You remind me every day that God is good and grace is true.*
*You make life fun—even the parts that need a lot of hacking.*

# ACKNOWLEDGMENTS

It takes a good-sized village to create authors and make books. Consequently, I want to thank:

- Mrs. Burlew and Mrs. Slattery for teaching me to read.

- Mom, for taking me to the library week after week.

- Mrs. Charlotte Rogers, for patiently teaching me how to type.

- Professor Howard Hendricks, for encouraging me to be creative.

- Frederick Buechner, for showing me how piercing and powerful words can be.

- Dave Veerman, for giving me so many chances and opening so many doors.

- Steve Laube, for introducing me to Todd Hafer.

- Todd Hafer, for believing in this idea and guiding this project.

- Harvest House, for the opportunity to partner in such a fun endeavor.

- Kim Moore and Jean Kavich Bloom, for all the editing expertise and encouragement.

- My family and friends, near and far, who encourage me every day to keep tending and tweaking and "hacking" my soul.

# CONTENTS

# FOREWORD
## BY DAVE VEERMAN

've known Len Woods for almost 40 years.

A gifted writer, Len pulls you in and keeps you engaged, communicating profound truths in ways that almost anyone can understand. A minister since his college days, he has worked with people of all ages in life's joys, struggles, challenges, and growing pains, helping them mature in the faith. A practical practitioner, he knows how to help readers see themselves in the Bible and understand how to apply its principles.

*Spiritual Life Hacks* brings it all together: Len's passion for God's truth, his sensitivity to people and their life issues, his practical wisdom, and his writing ability.

These "hacks" begin with real issues faced by real people—and you may find that some of these situations will make you say, "That's me!" Then Len gives intensely practical and hopeful suggestions for helping resolve these common problems. His answers are simple but not simplistic. They're clear and concise.

So many of these hacks spoke to me, but I was especially challenged by the last one—"When You're Wondering, *How Long Will I Need to Keep Hacking My Heart?*"—and Len's powerful conclusion.

situation and the next and then the next. Keep pen and paper alongside as you read—you'll want to keep a list of hacks to take with you through the day. As you do what Len suggests, I'm convinced you will experience life change.

ENJOY!

*Dave*

**Dave Veerman** is a cocreator of the bestselling *Life Application Study Bible* and award-winning author of more than 70 books, including *Tough Parents for Tough Times, 365 Pocket Morning Prayers*, and *Unwrapping the Bible*.

# WHAT THE HECK IS A "HACK"?

*ack.*

Everything about the word makes us wince. Its primary meaning—"to cut or sever with repeated irregular or unskillful blows"[1]—sounds like a scene from a horror movie.

Then there was that time somebody figured out your sophisticated password system ("qwerty" for everything), *hacked* into your home Wi-Fi network, and used your credit card to go flat-panel TV shopping in Omsk, Russia. And the time you nearly *hacked* up a lung during a bout with the flu. And let's not forget that "nice handyman" you hired to install a new power outlet in the kitchen. Because he was a YouTube-educated *hack*—not a certified electrician—your bathroom light switch now opens the garage door.

Have no fear. Our focus here is on a different, more positive kind of *hack*.

In the mid-1950s and early '60s, the word *hack* became a badge of honor at highbrow institutions like Harvard and MIT. A *hack* was what engineering and computer whizzes called an inventive work-around, a creative fix to a technical problem. A *hacker* was any clever person who demonstrated skill at solving technological problems—often in a mischievous, non-malicious way.

Who is the world's most famous hacker? The person who brought innovative problem solving into the mainstream? That's easy—the fictional star of the ABC series *MacGyver*, which aired from 1985–1992.[2]

Angus "Mac" MacGyver worked for a secret government agency as well as a think tank called the Phoenix Foundation. He was the anti-James Bond. Unsophisticated. Not at all suave—he wore a mullet haircut, drove a jeep, and loved hockey. MacGyver didn't carry a gun, just his trusty Swiss Army knife. Because he was whip-smart and more resourceful than a whole troop of Eagle Scouts, he could turn everyday objects into gizmos that would save the day. Once he used a gearshift knob, some stuffing from a seat cushion, a cigarette lighter, and a muffler to build a rocket-propelled grenade (RPG) he successfully fired into the radiator of the car that was chasing him!

For a whole generation of techno-nerdy TV viewers, the name MacGyver became a verb: "So I grabbed my duct tape, a couple of empty two-liter soda bottles, and my flashlight, and I MacGyvered all that into a hands-free headlamp."

Nowadays, any MacGyver-ish fix to an everyday problem is called a *life hack*. All over the internet, insightful "life hack gurus"— we used to call such people "grandparents"—have created websites devoted to *life hacking*. They're making stacks of cash showing people tips like:

- How to use an old sunscreen bottle to hide their valuables at the beach.

- How to keep their cats from unrolling the toilet paper.

- How to cut a cake using dental floss. (Seriously. People do this. I guess so they won't have to spend ten whole seconds washing that big old knife? Or maybe the thought is that by flossing the cake first, they won't need to floss their teeth later? Whatever. Just know that if you decide to try this hack, you'll want to go with non-minty floss.)

Clearly, some popular life hacks are Shakespearean—as in, much ado about nothing. But other hacks *can* enhance your life. Who doesn't want that?

Leon Ho, the CEO and founder of lifehack.org (one of those aforementioned websites), has defined a life hack as "practical, actionable knowledge that can immediately boost one aspect of your life."[3] He says that when you apply needed hacks to multiple problems, "you will start seeing big improvements in your overall quality of life."[4]

Sounds inviting, doesn't it? If you can show me a creative way to eliminate a pesky problem, an overlooked trick for saving money or time, or an innovative way to not only reduce frustration but make life more enjoyable? I'm all in. Let's start hacking!

But for people of faith, that raises the question of *spiritual* life hacks. Is there such a thing? Are there out-of-the-box fixes for out-of-kilter souls?

Yes and yes.

Before we look at some, though, a couple of disclaimers are in order.

# 1. THERE'S A BIG DIFFERENCE BETWEEN A LIFE HACK AND A SPIRITUAL LIFE HACK

If you're frustrated because you can never seem to find the end of a roll of shipping tape, I have good news: There's a quick life hack for that! Press a paper clip onto the sticky side of the tape right at the end of the roll. Voila! MacGyver would be proud! Now your future taping sessions will be a breeze instead of a headache.

But what if your problem is more complicated, more personal? What if, let's say, you become a nervous wreck every time you think about your uncertain future? That calls for a different kind of hack, as the following chart shows:

| LIFE HACKS... | SPIRITUAL LIFE HACKS... |
| --- | --- |
| ...address problems on the surface of one's life (e.g., removing debris from my computer keyboard). | ...target issues at the core of one's being (e.g., confronting paralyzing fear in your soul). |
| ...focus on technology, efficiency, and productivity. | ...focus on spirituality, humanity, and mystery. |
| ...are often quick, simple, one-time actions. | ...typically require repetition, a longer process, or the formation or cessation of a habit. |
| ...make life more convenient in the short-term. | ...make life more meaningful for the long-term. |
| ...are about being clever. | ...are about becoming the person God made you to be. |

## 2. SOME INFORMATION HERE MIGHT
## SOUND FAMILIAR—AND THAT'S ON PURPOSE

One of the realities of living in the information age is that human knowledge is now growing exponentially. While our desire to learn new things is commendable, the Bible also warns against the danger of forgetting old truths. Spiritually speaking, it's possible to become people who, in the apostle Paul's words, are "always learning but never able to come to a knowledge of the truth" (2 Timothy 3:7).

I'm like you. When I pick up a new book or listen to a speaker, I'm subconsciously thinking, *Tell me something fresh and interesting. Tell me a fascinating story or explain a life-changing truth I've never heard or never quite understood.* (Trust me, as a full-time writer and sometimes speaker, I feel immense pressure to be original and creative. Every communicator wants to ferret out and offer up some brilliant pearl of wisdom nobody in the history of history has ever thought or expressed.)

However, I'm also reminded of Solomon's wise observation about there being "nothing new under the sun" (Ecclesiastes 1:9). I think, too, of the insightful words of the scholar Samuel Johnson: "People need to be reminded more often than they need to be instructed." Maybe this, as one old preacher said, is why the Bible has only about eight big ideas that God keeps repeating again and again.[5]

Needing reminders—that's been *my* experience. And I'm convinced I'm not alone. We all need regular reminders because we're all expert forgetters!

If I can share both some helpful information that's new *and* a few crucial reminders in these pages, all in a clear and creative way, my prayers will have been answered.

# Spiritual Life Hacks

# 1

# WHEN YOU'RE WONDERING WHERE TO START HACKING

f you've seen the classic movie *The Princess Bride*, you probably remember the villain Vizzini's repeated use of the word *inconceivable*. And you recall the swordsman Inigo Montoya's classic response: "You keep using that word. I do not think it means what you think it means."

Inigo could have said the same thing about our use of the word *heart*. We toss that word around the way politicians throw out promises during election season. In any given week, we read about assorted *heartaches* on Facebook. We drink coffee with a friend who has *a heavy heart*. We lament the relational woes of the neighbors: She loves him *with all her heart*, but he's *cold-hearted* toward her.

The *heart* is a staple of our music: *How can you mend a broken heart?* the Bee Gees mourned even as the great Tony Bennett crooned about how he *left his heart* in San Francisco. (Maybe that's how one becomes *heartless?*)

Somebody—hopefully not a cardiac surgeon—declared, "The way to a man's heart is through his stomach." Alas, you can *open your heart, pour out your heart,* and *wear your heart on your sleeve.* (Maybe this explains, in part, how hearts get *crushed* and *hardened.*)

You get the point. Our culture talks a lot about the "heart." But does the word mean what we think it means?

The Bible contains about a thousand references to the heart.[1] In most of these instances, the word is used metaphorically. According to the Good Book, your heart is your invisible, immaterial essence— some would say your soul or human spirit. It's that knot of intangibles—personality, likes, dislikes, beliefs, desires, and so on—that makes you uniquely you.

Thus, the Bible sees the heart as both the repository and the driver of all of our rich and quirky humanness, in at least three primary ways.

First, the heart is where we *feel* (Psalm 34:18; Proverbs 15:13; Romans 9:2). Your *heart* is where you experience pleasant emotions like love and euphoria, where you healthily process (or unhealthily bury) painful experiences. Nostalgia, regret, sadness, old wounds, and joyful memories are all rooted in the heart.

Second, the heart is where we *think* (1 Kings 3:9; Proverbs 15:14; 23:7). Perhaps you're saying, "Wait a minute—aren't you confusing the heart with the mind?" The answer is no. The ancient Hebrews didn't draw a sharp distinction between the heart and the mind the way we do in modern Western culture.

If you conducted a survey, most people would say, "Our 'mind' is our analytical side, whereas our 'heart' is our touchy-feely side." If you pressed them, they'd articulate a dichotomy something like this:

| MIND | HEART |
|:---:|:---:|
| Calculating | Impulsive |
| Responsible | Risky |
| Logic | Love |
| A science book | A romance novel |
| Algebra II | Art class |
| Concrete | Abstract |
| Scientific | Sentimental |
| Rational | Irrational |
| An engineering degree | A humanities degree |

That's how modern Western culture thinks. But this sharp distinction between the mind and the heart isn't found in the Bible because in ancient Near Eastern cultures, the intellectual and emotional blurred and overlapped. (This no doubt explains why the biblical writers often use the terms *mind* and *heart* interchangeably.)

All this to say that, biblically speaking, your heart isn't just where you "get the feels." It's also where you analyze and evaluate. With your heart you rigorously discern, ponder, and wrestle with assorted ideas. Your unique attitudes and opinions, your personal values, your beliefs and convictions are all rooted in your heart.

Third, the Bible sees the heart as the place where we *decide* (Deuteronomy 30:10; Proverbs 5:12; Acts 11:23). Your heart is where you resolve to move in a certain direction or choose to engage in this action but not that one. Intentions, willingness, ambitions, and goals are all rooted in your heart.

This explains why the heart is such a monumental topic in the Bible! It's our central essence; our feeler, thinker, and chooser; the command and control center of our lives. No wonder wise King Solomon said, "Above all else, guard your heart, for everything you do flows from it" (Proverbs 4:23).

Why should our hearts be top priority? Because, as Solomon pointed out, the condition of our hearts determines the direction of our lives.

Jesus put it this way: "A good person produces good things from the treasury of a good heart, and an evil person produces evil things from the treasury of an evil heart" (Luke 6:45 NLT). In other words, if our hearts aren't right, nothing else about our lives will be right.

Life's little irritations can often be hacked in a flash: Got assorted computer cables and charger cords that keep falling behind your desk? A few large bulldog clips can help you organize them and keep them within easy reach.

What about when your problems are trickier? Like when…

- You realize you've developed an unusually short fuse. (Little annoyances that typically don't bother you suddenly have you barking at the kids and bristling at your coworkers.)

- The bottom drops out of your faith.

- Your best friend calls with terrible news.

- You spend a few minutes on social media and come away feeling critical, envious, angry, bummed out, or some messy combination of all that.

- You find yourself wanting to pull back from relationships that were once high priority to you.

- The people at your new job are driving you nuts.

In those kinds of situations, you're going to need more than a coat hanger and an old empty milk jug. You'll have to go to the root of the problem. You'll have to start with your heart.

Suppose that in looking within, you realize your soul is badly out of whack. What then? Has God left you to figure out this heart hack stuff by yourself?

Inconceivable.

## 2

# WHEN YOU FEEL DISILLUSIONED BY YOUR LACK OF SPIRITUAL GROWTH

Before we dive headlong into a bunch of spiritual life hacks, I probably ought to give you a quick spiritual history of my own life.

I'm from the Deep South—that region of the USA Flannery O'Connor once described as "hardly Christ-centered [but] most certainly Christ-haunted."[1] Growing up to a steady stream of sermons about hell and the Holy Ghost, I was *definitely* Christ-haunted.

As a child I asked Jesus to "come into my life" almost daily. Each Sunday my family attended church, where I dutifully put my "tithe" (a tenth of my 25 cents weekly allowance) in the offering plate.[2] I was baptized at age seven, a second time at age 12. My teenage years were a blur of schoolwork and leisure suits, hormones and guilt, all punctuated by "rededicating my life to Christ" every two or three months.

During my first semester of college, something unexpected and mysterious happened in my soul. I was at a weekend retreat, and it was as if God nudged me awake from a deep slumber and invited me to go on a long journey.

Overflowing with spiritual excitement and curiosity, I started frequenting Bible studies the way most college students barhop. I went on mission projects. I started talking about my faith to strangers. In a campus ministry, I even taught some classes about the basics of the Christian faith. (In my "free time," I somehow earned a degree in journalism.)

After graduation, I became the world's most incompetent youth director. (The fact that no one sued me for ministerial malpractice during those three years is borderline miraculous.) I moved to Texas and got a master's degree in theology. I married a remarkable woman, and I helped launch a magazine designed to get teenagers reading the Bible. Then, for the next 24 years, I reared two sons, pastored two congregations, and wrote extensively about God and faith, the Bible and life. During these assorted life chapters, I experienced moments when God's presence and love were palpable. But I experienced lots of other periods when God seemed more like an imaginary friend.

I think back over my odd spiritual journey, and I'm thankful but also filled with questions: Why, after four-plus decades, don't I have more faith and joy? Why is it still so hard for me to love certain people? By now, shouldn't I have a better handle on anger and worry, insecurity and envy? Shouldn't I be further along? Why am I not more like Christ?

Sometimes I look at my lack of progress and become seriously disillusioned.

Maybe you feel that way too.

What if I told you that feeling like that—spiritually disillusioned—is a *good* thing, not a *bad* thing?

Here's why that's true: The prefix *dis* means "without or separated from." Being *disinherited* means your parents (or their attorneys) tell you to plan on living the rest of your life *without* any family money (not a cause for celebration). Being *disemboweled* means someone *separates* your innards from the rest of your body (not medically recommended).

*Disillusioned* means being "without illusions." Meaning, a *disillusioned* person has been separated from fictitious thoughts and made-up beliefs. In other words, being disillusioned is getting a ticket from fantasyland back to reality.

Isn't that something we should all seek?

One of the most common illusions held by Christians (especially new believers) is that spiritual transformation typically happens via sporadic, dramatic experiences. In a personal prayer time or at a big worship service, let's say, or while reading a dynamic Christian book or attending camp or sitting at a Bible conference, God suddenly jolts you. You have an ecstatic experience that transcends words. This notion of spiritual growth goes on to say that if you can just have enough spiritual experiences like this, over time your faith and spiritual life will grow stronger.

We likely get this idea from reading about the apostle Paul's miraculous encounter with the resurrected Jesus on the Damascus Road (Acts 9) or Isaiah's soul-shaking vision of God in the temple (Isaiah 6). We think, *THAT is how it's supposed to happen. I need God to come crashing into my life like THAT. A few experiences like THAT, and nothing would ever be the same. My prayers would suddenly have new power. I'd start seeing bona fide miracles on a regular basis. I'd instantly be freed from my self-centered attitude and my critical spirit.*

*I'd love everyone and everything—maybe even cats and polka music. (Okay, maybe not the cat part.)*

If you think I sound like I'm mocking, forgive me. I'm *not* for one moment suggesting that God Almighty can't supernaturally "zap" people and initiate sudden, dramatic changes in their lives. *Of course* he can do that—and thankfully, he *does* do that on occasion.[3]

What I *am* saying is that the Bible presents such encounters as the exception, not the rule. Nowhere does Scripture tell us to passively wait for "holy, heavenly lightning" to strike our souls. In short, it's an illusion to think that significant and permanent spiritual progress normally comes via random, one-time actions or experiences. It's true that I can place my iPhone in an empty drinking glass—the operative word being *empty*—and the music coming out of its tiny speakers will suddenly be amplified. It's *not* true that I can mystically put Bibles all around my house and suddenly hear God's voice in a clearer, louder way. That's not how the spiritual life works.

How does the spiritual life work? One of the best biblical statements about what we mean when we talk about hacking our spiritual life is found in a first-century letter the apostle Paul wrote to his young protégé Timothy. While giving Timothy some practical counsel about living in a godless culture, the wise old saint urged, "Train yourself to be godly" (1 Timothy 4:7).

Here's why this command is so fascinating: The Greek word translated "train" is the word from which we get our English word *gymnasium.* Reading this sentence, Timothy would have immediately thought of athletes *exercising!*

*Train* is a verb that reeks of sweat. It's a workout word. Think of a weight room—all those loud grunts, all those iron plates clanging together, panting athletes barking encouragement to one another.

Guess what? Those athletes aren't under the illusion that they can do one superintense workout today and then kick back for the rest of the season. No, they'll be back tomorrow and the next day and the day after that. That's because inherent in the term *training* is the idea of *habitual.* Athletes in training *keep showing up* to work out—not sporadically but *regularly.* That's the only way to gain strength and endurance, and it's the only way to keep them. Why does the star basketball player shoot free throws for an extra hour after practice *every day*? So that in the big game, when the score is tied with one second left on the clock, she can confidently step to the line and swish the game-winning foul shot.

Athletes train *all the time* in order to reach their full potential. Paul is saying Christians need to do the same. While it's true that God is the only one who can truly transform a heart, we have a vital part to play. We're called to "work out our salvation" even as God does his work *in* us (Philippians 2:12-13). Godliness, or becoming like Jesus, isn't, then, the result of a "zap." To be sure, we need God's transforming touch, but life change also requires work and effort on our part. We can't be passive; we must keep showing up. To think otherwise is to live under an *illusion.*

Christians often refer to this kind of spiritual training as engaging in spiritual disciplines or practices or exercises. We can call them holy habits, or we can even call them heart hacks. What we call them is irrelevant. What matters is that we do them regularly, constantly—like those pro golfers who take an annoying number of practice swings before and after every shot or putt. When such acts—or hacks—become ingrained habits, a kind of way of life, we see slow, steady growth in faith. Let me say it again: If we remember to do them only once in a blue moon and expect to make spiritual progress, we're living under a giant illusion.

Spiritual hacks require consistency, but at least they're not complicated. They don't call for angels or heavenly visions. You don't need a seminary degree or lots of "spiritual equipment," and you surely don't have to be a monk or a mystic. Think of heart hacks as creative, yet down-to-earth ways of orienting your soul or angling your heart in a Godward direction. You can do them anywhere and at any time. They're not—and this is crucial to grasp—a way of winning favor with the Lord. We don't do them to impress God. We do them to be *with* God in the hopes that we will be *like* him one day.

If you've been operating under the illusory idea that you could be jolted into holiness if only you could pray the right prayer, or have the right conference experience, or attend the perfect worship service—or if you've always assumed that to make progress in the faith, all you have to do is log enough years in Sunday school—I'm here to disillusion you. Paul's command to Timothy (and to us) is "Train yourself to be godly."

In the chapters that follow, I'll introduce you to (or remind you of) some uncommon—some might say "off-the-wall"—spiritual life hacks. With a bit of effort and lots of help from above, these little actions can become holy habits. As such, they have the power to reshape your heart by continually opening it to the transforming presence of God.

Are you in? Other than a bunch of useless illusions, what have you got to lose?

3

# WHEN YOU'RE HEADING OUT INTO A PROBLEM-FILLED WORLD

Gather a bunch of life hackers. Ask them to name their most useful tool or resource. Chances are most will say, "Duct tape."

God bless duct tape![1] It's one of the Almighty's best gifts, one of mankind's greatest inventions. Developed during World War II, duct tape was initially used to keep ammunition boxes sealed and watertight. Since then, it's proven to be invaluable in all sorts of situations. With duct tape you can quickly patch leaky hoses, tents, and even canoes. In certain "wedding emergencies," you can use it to secure an unstitched trouser hem or wrap a piece around your hand (sticky side out) to create a last-minute lint roller. Nervous about people tripping over electrical cords at your big function? Got a wart you need to get rid of in a week?[2] Know some astronauts in peril on their mission to the moon?[3] No worries whatsoever—not if you have duct tape.

The older I get, the more I'm convinced there's an overlooked, one-word prayer in the Bible that's the "duct tape" of the spiritual life.

It's the cry "Hosanna!" found only in Gospel accounts of Jesus entering Jerusalem on what we call Palm Sunday (Matthew 21:9,15; Mark 11:9-10; John 12:13). Over and over, the boisterous, restless crowds lining the road yelled this word at Christ. Derived from a Hebrew verb found in Psalm 118:25, *hosanna* means "Save us, we pray!"

The idea of *salvation* in the Bible is like the topic of *income* in the U.S. tax code—it comes up everywhere. In the New International Version of the Bible (NIV), we find the word *save* or one of its sister words—*salvation, saved, Savior, saves, saving*—six hundred times!

In the broadest sense, *saved* means "rescued" or "delivered." Thus, oftentimes in the Bible, the salvation being requested or celebrated isn't even spiritual in nature; it's deliverance from physical perils: disease, disaster, or defeat by an enemy.

Yet the Bible is clear: Our need for rescue extends far beyond earthly jams. We need eternal deliverance. We need salvation from the gravest problem of all—being on the outs with God.

Genesis 3 describes the origins of humanity's biggest predicament—the first man and woman, crazy with pride, turning away from the One who is Life itself. When they did, they plunged the world into ruin, and then they passed on their flawed genes and rebellious natures. We're all affected, or afflicted, or infected. And whatever biblical metaphor we choose—straying sheep, wayward children, enemies of God, the "walking dead" (Isaiah 53:6; Luke 15:11-31; Romans 5:10; Ephesians 2:1-2)—this simple fact remains: We need rescue.

The Gospels present Jesus as that deliverer. His very name means "the Lord saves" (Matthew 1:21), and he described his mission this way: "For the Son of Man came to seek and to save the lost" (Luke 19:10).

You might be wondering, *Why this review of Gospel basics? Why so much fuss over the word* hosanna? Here's why: Because all too often we forget how vast and glorious the salvation of Jesus is.

The other day my wife and I got into a conversation with our friend Jessica. It began via text and then morphed into a lively phone call. We were discussing faith, specifically when we first believed— or when, as Christians in the Bible Belt often express it, we were "saved."

Because of all the heart-tugging sermons we heard, childhood prayers we said, and powerful spiritual experiences we had, none of us could pinpoint an exact moment. Finally, we settled on this: The next time someone asks us, "Are you saved?" we will respond, "Saved? Why, yes! I *have been* saved, I *am being* saved, and I *will be* saved."

This is our nod to the expansive way the Bible speaks of God's great salvation. The apostle Paul wrote about *justification* (Romans 3:21-26). This is the stunning truth that God, by his amazing grace, declares sinners righteous when they place their faith in Christ.[4] However, this rescue from sin's penalty isn't the end of God's all-encompassing salvation—it's only the beginning!

The Bible also talks extensively about *sanctification* (John 17:17 and Hebrews 10:14, for example). Derived from a verb that means "to set apart or make holy," this word has to do with God saving us from the power of sin in everyday life. Sanctification is what Christians are referring to when they speak of "spiritual growth," "maturing in the faith," "living a holy life," or "working out their salvation" (2 Peter 3:18; 1 Corinthians 14:20; 1 Peter 1:15; Philippians 2:12-13). In truth, sanctification is a messy, lifelong process in which we try to get our balky hearts to cooperate with the Holy Spirit so we can gradually become like Jesus (Philippians 1:6; Galatians 5:16-26). On a practical level, sanctification is God rescuing us daily from wrong thoughts, sinful urges, bad situations, and old, destructive habits.

Last, there's *glorification*—the culmination of God's great salvation. Glorification refers to the coming day when believers will be delivered not just from the penalty and power of sin but ultimately from sin's very presence. In the life to come, we'll see the Lord in all his glory, face-to-face. And as restored image bearers, we will reflect that radiant glory forever (Romans 8:29; 2 Corinthians 3:18; Philippians 3:21; 2 Timothy 2:10; 1 John 3:2).

All this rich truth makes *Hosanna!*—the one-word plea for salvation—a great hack. In the same way that it's smart to keep a roll of duct tape handy, we'd also be wise to stuff our pockets full of "hosannas" before we head out the door. Let's be honest. Who among us doesn't need to be rescued daily from a hundred different things?

The irrational worry over this. The crippling fear over that. The unhealthy relationship. The destructive habit. The flashing anger. The negative outlook. The alluring temptation. The powerful addiction. The pit of depression. The prison of shame. The mystery illness. The crisis at work... We could go on and on and on.

God can rescue us from such things. Clearly, he means to. Why else would he have sent his Son to die for us and his Spirit to live in us? Salvation isn't restricted to a spiritual experience from our past. And it doesn't just promise heaven when we die; it also means hope and power now.

Let's stop thinking of salvation only in historic or eventual terms. God can save us today—and in the most practical ways. Whether you whisper it or shout it, crying out "Hosanna!" to Jesus is an acknowledgment of two personal truths: 1) *I am a mess who happens to be in a mess*, and 2) *I believe you can deliver me.*

Want to be a world-class hacker? Do two things: (1) Stick a roll a duct tape in your glove compartment, and (2) add the word *Hosanna!* to your spiritual vocabulary and use it until you're blue in the face.

# WHEN YOU CAN'T SEE GOD WORKING IN YOUR LIFE

Most kids can't tell you what they want for lunch, but after watching classic animated films like *Toy Story* and *The Lion King*, Richie knew what he wanted to do for the rest of his life. Realizing he could honor God, bless others, and bring joy to his own soul through making movies, Richie got busy. He started shooting and editing funny videos with his younger siblings. In college he earned a fine arts degree in 3-D animation.

With diploma in hand and a million creative ideas swirling in his heart, Richie was ready to take Tinsel Town by storm. He began tossing his résumé around Hollywood like confetti.

The result?

Silence.

Richie was undeterred. He scoured the internet nightly for new job postings. To pay bills, he took a job mowing grass at a local golf course from 5 a.m. to 3 p.m. daily. Each afternoon—after ten hours at work—he'd play a few holes of golf with his granddad, and together they would pray for God to open a door. After months of mowing, praying, applying, and waiting…mowing, praying, applying, and waiting…

Crickets. (Unfortunately, none of them with connections to *Jiminy*, the world's most famous animated cricket.)

Don't you sometimes wonder what in the world God is doing? Admit it. In your darkest moments, don't you question if he's doing anything at all? You're in a tough spot. You bombard heaven with all sorts of raw, desperate prayers, endlessly begging the Almighty to show up, help, give relief—to do *something*. Anything.

Nothing changes.

What are we supposed to do when there's no visible proof God is working in our lives?

I'll tell you what I do. I think about a short Bible passage in the first part of Exodus.[1] Most people overlook these verses in their rush to get to the more thrilling story of God calling out to Moses from the midst of a burning bush, telling him to go back to Egypt and lead the Israelites to freedom.

Big mistake.

Here's the passage we too often skim past:

> During that long period…the Israelites groaned in their slavery and cried out, and their cry for help because of their slavery went up to God. God heard their groaning and he remembered his covenant with Abraham, with Isaac and with Jacob. So God looked on the Israelites and was concerned about them. Now Moses was tending the flock of Jethro his father-in-law…and came to Horeb, the mountain of God." (Exodus 2:23–3:1).

I *love* this little section of Scripture. I think about how "during

that long period," the captive Israelites could see only the grim realities directly in front of them: the brutality of their Egyptian captors,
the hopeless faces of their children, the fact that despite their frantic,
fervent prayers,[2] no relief was anywhere on the horizon.

What they couldn't see, of course, was into heaven. There was no
way for them to look up and see God looking down on them with
concern. No way to see that God *was* aware of their pain, that he
*was* at work on a plan that would bring about their rescue. No way
to see that coming day when Moses would suddenly show back up
in Egypt, confront Pharaoh, and lead them to freedom.

And Moses? His view wasn't much better. As far as he could see,
his best opportunities were behind him. A long time before in a
world far, far away, he'd clumsily attempted to save his people, only
to end up fleeing Egypt like a scalded dog. As a result, Moses had
resigned himself to living out his days in obscurity, chasing flocks
of stupid sheep in circles around the desert. No way could he see
the burning bush just ahead or the fact that the final years of his life
would be his best years by far.

The story of Moses is primarily about how God saved the Jewish
people to bring ultimate salvation to the entire world. But a smaller
takeaway from that story is that *we can't always see the good things
God is up to.*

Jesus said it clearly: God is *always* working (John 5:17). Doesn't
it seem that an infinite God would have an uncountable number of
projects going on all the time?

Our problem, however, is this: Of the countless ways the
Almighty is working at any given moment, we're lucky if we can
see two or three of them.[3] Even as I type and you read this sentence,

we're not privy to how the Lord is orchestrating situations and synchronizing the schedules of people to accomplish his purposes.

We can't, for instance, see the discussions taking place in some distant office. Or the life-changing email that will arrive next Wednesday. Or all the seemingly random decisions, one after another, that will put a new friend or a potential spouse or a fresh business associate directly in our path next summer. Tell me, what scared soul can see how the dark path they're walking today will lead to unimaginable blessing in the future?

But just because we can't *see* those things doesn't mean they won't eventually happen.

What's the hack here? Is there one? You bet!

Sometimes when I can't see what God is up to, I curl my thumb and fingers around like a kid holding an invisible spyglass. Then I raise my hand to my eye and peer out at the world.

It's silly, I know, but this simple, childlike gesture helps me remember that my view of reality is and always will be extremely limited, like looking through a peephole or peering through a knothole in a fence.

Sometimes I don't even go to the trouble of pulling out my fancy spyglass. I just stare out the window above my desk. It's a smallish window facing north, blocked on the west by a big Ligustrum hedge. From my chair, I can see exactly two and a half homes and 19 trees. That's all. But I let that limited view remind me of the innumerable ways God is at work beyond my tiny field of vision.

Back to the creative kid who wanted to make movies... We left him praying and waiting. Whatever happened to Richie?

One humdrum day while he was—you guessed it—mowing, his cell phone buzzed in his pocket. It was a movie studio calling—and not just any studio, but DreamWorks![4] Richie almost fell off his tractor.

The recruiters at DreamWorks said they were extremely impressed with his résumé, and they wanted to know if he could fly to California for an interview. (His family agreed later that he probably could have flown without an aircraft!)

The visit could not have gone better. Afterward, Richie felt exceedingly hopeful about his chances. Talk about childhood dreams coming true!

But a few days passed.

Then a few more.

Richie heard nothing—not a word.

Until the ho-hum afternoon he and his grandfather were engaged in their daily "play and pray" golf ritual. Richie's phone buzzed again. It was DreamWorks calling to offer him an animation job!

Sitting in their golf cart, Richie and his granddad wept for joy.

One recent Saturday night, I flicked on the TV just in time to see the end of the movie *Cast Away*. The film stars Tom Hanks as Chuck Noland, a FedEx executive who survives an air crash at sea and ends up stranded all alone on a remote island—for *four years*!

When (spoiler alert!) a large piece of a portable toilet washes ashore, desperate Chuck gets an idea. He builds a ramshackle raft, using the fiberglass as a makeshift sail. After a harrowing journey toward the shipping lanes, Chuck is spotted by a merchant vessel and rescued. Arriving back home in Memphis, he's devastated to learn that his fiancée has moved on and married someone else. Faced with the prospect of rebuilding his entire life, a somber Chuck sighs and tells a friend—and his own soul—what he must do: "I gotta keep breathing. Because tomorrow the sun will rise. Who knows what the tide could bring?"

There you have it. When we can't see God working, the hack we need is to look through our knothole again and keep breathing. Mow another fairway. Fill out another application. Check the beach one more time. Keep praying, waiting, and trusting. Trust that just beyond the range of our pitiful, invisible spyglasses, God is orchestrating things.

*All* things.

He's co-opting the ocean currents and commandeering the common bushes of life. He's working in and through the prayers of granddads and the skittish hearts of reluctant leaders. Nothing, not even a slow-moving HR department, can thwart his will! At just the right moment, usually when we least expect it, the cell phone *will* buzz.

Who knows what the tide could bring indeed?

## 5

# WHEN YOU'RE BATTLING DOUBTS

know a woman (let's call her Annie) who recently worked up the courage to admit the deep, uncomfortable truth of her soul to some of her closest Christian friends—she is drowning in doubt.

Her faith, which used to sparkle and stun like a ravishing bride on her wedding day, now looks haggard, more like a runaway bride after a sleepless, 53-hour, cross-country bus trip. Real life and church life, God and evil, science and the Bible… Annie isn't sure how to fit it all together. She doesn't know *what* she believes—or some days, if she believes at all.

Annie's not a heretic—not what Scripture would call a scoffer or mocker. She's not running around talking derisively about the gospel or trying to turn people away from God. In truth, she wants desperately to believe. But troubling questions without simple answers keep bubbling up in her soul. For the longest time, she just shoved down the questions, which proved to be exhausting. Then, because hiding such realities from close friends felt so dishonest, Annie decided to be authentic, to come clean. You know, spill the spiritual beans.

Annie's friends were caught off guard. Her transparency obviously made them uncomfortable, because they immediately became defensive. When Annie tried to explain herself more clearly, the tension only escalated. The friends, either forgetting or ignorant of the biblical command to "be merciful to those who doubt" (Jude 22), became preachy. For ten or fifteen minutes, with red faces and quavering voices, they chided Annie, lobbing Bible verses at her like hand grenades.

She immediately regretted her openness. (Later she thought that they might have been kinder if she'd confessed to robbing a convenience store.)

It's been said that 90 percent of all Christians have doubts, and the other 10 percent have a problem being honest about their doubts. That about sums it up. We are doubting believers, or believing doubters, depending on the day. For all (truthful) Christians, doubt is an occasional problem, and for some Christians, doubt is an all-the-time reality.

To clarify, *doubt* isn't limited to "questioning the existence of God" or "having misgivings about the Bible." Doubt is so much broader than that. When I'm not really convinced of God's love for me, when I'm skeptical that he can bring good out of bad, when I'm not so sure that he's with me or that he will provide for me—those are all examples of doubt rearing its head.

Of course, every act of sin has its roots in doubt. It's been this way since Eden. I remind you that Adam and Eve didn't eat the forbidden fruit until they first began to question God's motives. We defy

God's will because we doubt his heart. Of course we do; we're sons and daughters of the original doubting couple!

If we define doubt as "wavering faith in God in any given situation," who among us doesn't qualify as a doubter? Abraham, the great "father of faith," was a doubter. He famously doubted God's promise of offspring—with the result that he signed off on Sarah's half-baked plan to use her maid as a surrogate (Genesis 16). On two occasions, doubting that God could or would keep him safe, Abraham shamefully tried to pawn off his wife as his sister (Genesis 12:10-20; Genesis 20).

David had lapses in faith during which he lobbed doubt-filled questions at God (Psalm 13:1; 22:1). Even John the Baptist, who loudly declared to massive crowds that Jesus was the promised Messiah, later had some *I'm-not-so-sure* second thoughts while languishing in Herod's prison (Matthew 11:1-19; Luke 7:18-35). Peter, questioning the Lord's power to save and sustain him, denied even knowing Jesus (Matthew 26:69-75; Mark 14:66-72; Luke 22:54-62; John 18:16-18,25-27). Matthew admitted that some of the apostles, *when face-to-face with the resurrected Christ*, wrestled with doubt (Matthew 28:17).

All this encourages me as I try to "fight the good fight of the faith" (1 Timothy 6:12). I don't question the existence of God or doubt that Jesus came and did everything the Bible says he did. My doubts are more personal: Can all that really be true for me? Especially after I've pushed God away for the ten millionth time? Even when big parts of my heart remain so unchanged?

"A hack! A hack!" every desperate doubter yells. "My kingdom for a hack!"

Here's what I do—and what I suggest you do—when your faith is shaky and doubts start surging in your heart. Go to these three A-B-Cs:

1. *Accept that doubt is a universal phenomenon.* As we've seen, even the "All-Stars of the Faith" had their faithless moments. Because we have "under-construction" hearts and we live in a fallen world, why would an occasional attack of doubt shock anyone?

I get that most Christians are reluctant to admit a faltering faith (no doubt because they fear they'll get the response Annie got[1]). But pretending and living in denial aren't healthy. One of my favorite Bible characters is the unnamed man in Mark 9 whose child was dying and whose faith was on life support. He confessed honestly to Jesus, "I do believe; help me overcome my unbelief!" (verse 24). That's a prayer I offer up to God on *lots* of days.

Bottom line, you're *not* weird if you have doubts, and when you do have them, you *don't* have to be afraid to admit them to the Lord.

2. *Be merciful to yourself.* "Be merciful to those who doubt," Jude 22 tells us. This would seem to include being merciful to ourselves. While our fierce struggles with doubt don't exactly fill us with joy, they also shouldn't trigger a round of self-loathing. Resist the urge to beat yourself up. Remember that you're not a finished work (yet), so cut yourself some slack. (And ask God—or maybe since we're in the *B* part of this hack, *beseech* him—to give you at least one merciful Christian friend or mentor you can confide in.)

3. *Cling.* Cling stubbornly to the truth of God and let go of everything else. (As somebody once wisely urged, "Believe your beliefs and doubt your doubts.") Personally, I like to hang on to the comforting reminder of Psalm 63:8: The One to whom I cling is holding *me* in his big, strong right hand! Or you can grab hold of the promise of Philippians 1:6: The One who began the work of faith in your heart *will* finish it.

Until then, as Frederick Buechner said, doubts are just "the ants in the pants of faith. They keep it awake and moving."

# 6

# WHEN YOU FEEL OVERWHELMED

Question: What does Abby, who's getting married in three weeks, have in common with Ben, who just got laid off? (And the 500-point bonus question: What do the two of them have in common with the Garcias, who just bought a fixer-upper starter home?)

Answer: They could all use a good *list*.

David Wallechinsky, coauthor of the bestselling *Book of Lists* (and numerous sequels), says, "The everyday lists we all make are a balm to a cluttered mind."[1]

Everybody knows you don't have to be tying the knot, job hunting, or gutting an old kitchen to feel overwhelmed. Life comes at us faster and faster, offering more options than ever. It's said that grocery stores now offer 40,000 more items than they did just 20 years ago.

No wonder we feel the need to create lists of all kinds: shopping lists, to-do lists, "honey do" lists—if not on paper, then at least in our smartphones or heads. List making helps us sort through endless possibilities and settle on a few necessities. Lists provide order, clarity, focus, and motivation. By making life a bit more manageable, lists have a calming effect. A good list functions like a bouncer—it tells random or irrelevant items, "Sorry. Feel free to try to elbow your way into someone else's life, but you're not welcome here—not today."

In addition to being helpful, lists can make life more enjoyable. Doesn't your mood lift when you think back over your five best vacations or your ten favorite movies? This must be the reason author Umberto Eco once gushed, "There is nothing more wonderful than a list."

Because we're so fascinated by lists, whole websites—like list verse.com—do nothing but compile and curate lists. Best burgers in your state? Cheapest places to live? Most stressful occupations? Most popular baby names? Documented cases of people spontaneously combusting? If you can think of a category, I guarantee you there's a list for it somewhere on the internet.

What am I saying here? Simply this: List making is life enhancing. That's also true when we're trying to live by faith.

Praying, serving others, giving to the poor—these actions sound profoundly spiritual. But list making? It sounds so mundane.

And yet, have you noticed how many lists are in the Bible? The Good Book begins with a list of everything God created (Genesis 1). It ends with a narrative list of all the glories of heaven and eternity (Revelation 21–22).

In between we find the tribes of Israel listed (Numbers 1; 26), lists of things God hates (Proverbs 6:16-19), lists of spiritual virtues (Galatians 5:22-23)—even a list of building materials needed for the ancient Jewish tabernacle (Exodus 25–30). Scripture contains lists of apostles (Matthew 10:2-4), wise sayings (the book of Proverbs), and various spiritual abilities God has given believers to help build his church (1 Corinthians 12:1-11; Romans 12).

We could reference numerous other biblical lists, such as kosher and nonkosher foods (Leviticus 11), all the places the Israelites camped during their lengthy trip to the promised land (Numbers 33), and the lists of all the kings they defeated once they got there (Joshua 12). And let's not forget the most famous list in the history of the world—the Ten Commandments (Exodus 20).

The Bible contains all these lists because life—even the spiritual life—often becomes cluttered and confusing, and because good, concise lists have a way of helping us stay laser focused on what's important.

I submit to you that list making is an ingenious way to hack your heart. When you're starting to feel overwhelmed, you can make countless lists that will improve your outlook.

Let me list (ha-ha) just a few of the lists you might consider making:

- *My "Mount Rushmore" of Spiritual Mentors*—After you list these individuals, call, visit, or write them. Thank them for their investment in your life.

- *My Favorite Chapters in the Bible*—After listing them, prayerfully reread them a chapter a day.

- *Four Impossible Things I'm Trusting God For*—Post your list where you can see and pray for these items daily. Also, you might want to write the following verses across the top of this list: "Is anything too hard for the LORD?"

(Genesis 18:14), and "Everything is possible with God" (Mark 10:27 NLT).

- *Books of the Bible I Still Need to Read*—List them, read them, and then check them off one by one. (After all, you don't want Habakkuk to walk up to you in heaven and say, "How'd you like my book?" and have no clue. Talk about embarrassing!)

- *Five Bad Attitudes I'm Asking God to Help Me Change*— If, for example, one bad attitude is bitterness, spend a few appointments with God studying what the Bible says about bitterness, and keep asking the Lord for the grace to let go of any lingering resentments.

- *Seven Concrete Ways I Can Bless Seven Specific People in My Life This Coming Week*—Make your list, and then carry out the items one by one, a day at a time.

- *Things That Have Me Worried*—After listing everything you feel antsy or anxious about, divide your list into two sub-lists: "Situations I Have Some Control Over" and "Situations Beyond My Control." Start doing what you can to address the items in list #1. Offer the items in list #2 to God.

- *My Spiritual Bucket List*—Include spiritual classic books others have been encouraging you to read, experiences you'd like to have (a mission trip, visiting the Holy Land), and people with whom you'd like to have rich spiritual conversations.

Those are just a few ideas. No doubt you can come up with a better list of possible lists to make. All I can tell you is this little hack works like a charm. When you're feeling spiritually overwhelmed in some way, make a list and check it twice.

*7*

# WHEN LIFE IS FULL OF UNCERTAINTY

f you want to call this the Information Age, be my guest. I'm going with the more accurate Information Tsunami.

Every day I feel as if I'm being inundated by a *tidal wave* of fresh data, a flood of new insights, studies, and research. And for the record, I'm not imagining all this: IBM says we're close to the time when human knowledge will be doubling every 11 to 12 *hours!*[1]

No wonder my head hurts.

With each passing day, it's clear that I know less and less about more and more. At the rate I'm going, it's just a matter of time until I know nothing about everything. (Of course, the alternative isn't much better—all those specialists who keep learning more and more about less and less. Won't they eventually get to the place where they know everything about nothing?)

Here's the one thing about which I'm certain: You could fill the Pacific Ocean (and most of the Atlantic) with all the stuff I don't know, such as how "the cloud" works. Or why a sane person would choose a career in politics. Or why a coffee shop situated on a major interstate stops brewing dark roast coffee at 11 a.m. Or why our 28-year-old freezer has been making a *loud* clunking noise every 90 minutes for at least the past ten years.[2]

Silly trivialities aside, plenty of somber unknowns exist. The bad news du jour usually involves disease or disasters. What will we discover when we log on or tune in tomorrow? Something involving terrorists? Computer hackers? An economic meltdown? No "expert" on earth knows for sure.

Meanwhile, amid all that "Breaking News!" from a broken world, we face other uncertainties closer to home:

*What, if anything, can I do to repair my marriage?*
*What's going on in my child's heart?*
*If I lost this job, what would I do?*
*Does the dementia that runs in my family also run in me?*
*If I couldn't work anymore, how would we get by?*

Here's what's interesting: I bet you a cup of dark roast coffee (but only before 11 a.m.) that I could go online and, inside of five minutes, find a YouTube video that explains why my freezer is making a clunking sound. What I *can't* do—even with the exponential increase in human knowledge—is know what 2029 holds, or how much my Roth IRA will be worth in 15 years, or how many heartbeats I have left.

This ignorance explains why I've become so attached to a short phrase that's found in a few places in the Bible.[3] Israel's great kings—David and Solomon—used it, and so did prophets like Ezekiel and apostles like Peter.

The phrase is *you know*.

"You know."

We see it uttered in occasional prayers to God and in certain conversations with Jesus. Always, the people saying this phrase are facing uncertainty. They're in over their heads. They're feeling small, lost, and clueless about what to say or do next. Although it's only two words, "You know" is a mouthful. It's a way of humbly saying, "Don't ask me what's up, what's happening, or what's next. I don't know any of that. But, Lord, you do. You know. *You* know. You *know*."

Listen to the heart behind these two words, and you'll get the sense that the speaker is reckoning with a great truth: The One being addressed possesses all facts, sees every possible outcome, and knows without question the best way to proceed. In one sense, "You know" is a signal of humble resignation. Mostly, it's an expression of relief.

On his final night on earth, Jesus arranged to eat a farewell meal with the 12 apostles. Because he knew all that was just ahead, the Teacher elected to give one last lecture. As discourses go, this one was a doozy, a veritable tidal wave of truth. For the most part, the disciples listened quietly—though judging by the few, odd comments of Thomas, Philip, and Judas (not Judas Iscariot), it's clear none of them were tracking. Can we blame them? After such a strange and stressful week, the followers of Jesus were sure of only one thing: They weren't sure about much of anything.

I can imagine them in the candlelight, staring blankly at a platter of leftover lamb and bitter herbs, occasionally cutting their eyes toward one another. John admits they were whispering back and forth, "What does he mean?" "We don't understand what he's saying" (John 16:17-18). Thankfully, someone voiced to Jesus the one truth they all needed amid so much uncertainty: "*You know* all things" (verses 29-30, emphasis added).

Jesus let that statement linger, and then he told them to take heart. He prayed, and the meeting ended. They left the room, and just as he promised, all hell broke loose.

A week or two later, after the crucifixion and resurrection—those events happening exactly as Jesus knew and said they would—the Lord once again gathered with most of his closest followers (John 21). Peter, the de facto leader of the group and still wallowing in guilt for having failed Jesus in his hour of greatest need by denying him not once but three times,[4] was one of those present. Knowing precisely what the shame-filled apostle needed, Jesus asked Peter three consecutive times, "Do you love me?"

Jesus did this, by the way, not for his own information (he, of course, already knew the truth); he did it for Peter's restoration. Each time the humbled disciple insisted, "Lord, you know… Lord, you know… Lord, you know all things" (John 21:15-17).

What else was there to say?

"Lord, you know" has become one of my all-time favorite prayers. It's my go-to hack when I'm feeling clueless about my life or when I'm scared about what might be looming—which is to say, almost all the time.

My guess is that you're facing at least one situation where you don't know what's needed or what's coming. Maybe you're unsure about a next step. Or you're clear on the action you need to take but unclear about what might happen if you do. Perhaps you have perplexing questions: *What's troubling my child? Will I ever marry? How much longer do I have to endure this trial?*

I don't know much, but I can tell you this: When I say, "You know" to the only One who really *does* know, my jittery heart finds peace.

# 8

# WHEN YOU'RE KNACKERED

W hat American doesn't love to hear British people talk?
Their mesmerizing accents are, in large part, why James Bond seems so cool and why TV shows like *The Crown* and *Downton Abbey* are so popular. They are why in my BC days (Before Cindi), I once was smitten by four different British Airways flight attendants on a single transatlantic trip. (Note: I've been told the reason the English sound so refined is that they keep a stiff upper lip.)

Anyway, it's not only *how* Brits talk that's amazing; it's *what* they say. Other countries might be regarded as superior in culinary matters or in military strength, but when it comes to vocabulary, no one can compete with the English.

For example, we say "shocked," but they say "gobsmacked." We say "Shotgun!" or "Dibs!" and they cry "Bagsy!" Something that's a "failure" in Los Angeles is a "damp squib" in London.

And what about when British people feel exhausted from rattling off all these cool words and phrases? They don't say something lame like "I'm so tired." In England, they say, "I'm knackered."

Knackered.

We non-Brits might not use that word, but we feel the condition's effects. How could we not? Life hurtles on. At work, the projects stack up and the pressures intensify. At home, the to-do list lengthens and the Facebook feed never ends.

What, then, do we do? We get up a little earlier, and we stay up a little later. We multitask, doing more and more but enjoying life less and less. We need a break, but we can't stop, right? We push ahead. We keep going for fear we'll get left behind, perhaps even run over by all the people and demands breathing down our necks.

It's while we're in this depleted state that we're most inclined to become angry and exasperated, to say and do ridiculous, even irrational things. (The British call this "losing the plot"—a phrase which, in my opinion and in their vernacular, is "ace.")

Maybe you're in that place right now (not "ace" but "knackered"). You're out of gas. You have nothing left. And maybe the double whammy for you is that you think you can't come out and say that.

What a devilish lie. We fear that if we admit our struggles out loud, eyes will widen and eyebrows will rise. (In truth, they probably *would*, not because anything we're revealing—bitterness or envy or lust—is so rare but because being honest about such matters is.) The prospect of acknowledging "I'm knackered!" raises such fears. Who discloses feeling tired and weak but a weakling?

News flash: We're human beings. And while endurance and strength are praiseworthy traits, even Ironman triathletes can't go forever. God designed our bodies and minds to stop "doing" and go dormant for almost one-third of every day. He further instructed us to take every seventh day off—really "off."

Here's a thought: Maybe if we *feel* tired, it's because we *are* tired, and our feelings are simply in touch with reality. Maybe, because even machines made of steel wear out, we should stop feeling embarrassed when we get pooped out. Maybe, instead of feeling like a bunch of wimps, we should embrace our knackered-ness and receive God's good gifts of sleep and Sabbath with joy and gratitude.

Here's a hack for you, and it's decidedly nonclever: Listen to your knackered body and soul. Quit trying to be a macho man or Superwoman. Enough already with all the martyr talk ("If I don't do this, who will?"). Stop. Lie down. Close your eyes and rest. The world won't implode—you're not that essential.

If you won't take a nap, at least take a break. Walk outside, look up at the sky, and breathe deeply. Then walk back inside and look at your cluttered calendar, your stuffed schedule. Ask yourself, *What can I cut out?*

A passage in Matthew's Gospel shows Jesus talking to a big crowd of people. He didn't seem to be giving a formal message, such as his famous "Sermon on the Mount." This was more like a Q & A session—just him sharing his thoughts about a variety of topics. Then he spontaneously began to pray out loud. When he finished, he looked out at the crowd.

They were just…people. Regular folks like you and me. Moms worried about their kids. Dads wondering if they would be able to provide for their families. Some haunted by guilt, others reeling from grief or wallowing in depression or feeling blah about pretty much everything.

This world has a way of wearing us down and sucking the life right out of us. Everybody feels knackered at one time or another. Jesus knew that as well as anyone (Mark 4:38; John 4:6). Seeing that heaviness etched in their faces, Jesus gave one of his most famous invitations:

> Come to me, all you who are weary and burdened, and I will give you rest. Take my yoke upon you and learn from me, for I am gentle and humble in heart, and you will find rest for your souls. For my yoke is easy and my burden is light (Matthew 11:28-30).

Rest for the knackered. A sane, sensible life for those who have lost the plot. That's good news.

Or as the Brits would say, "Brilliant!"

# 9

# WHEN IT'S TAKING A LONG TIME TO BOUNCE BACK FROM A DRAINING EXPERIENCE

Good things take time," we're fond of saying. "Rome wasn't built in a day."

Yet even as we *say* such words, the high-energy, take-charge types in our midst are *thinking* very different thoughts: *For crying out loud! What's the holdup? Three monkeys could knock this out in ten minutes! Put ME in charge. Give me a good contractor and some cooperative weather, then get out of my way. I'll get "Rome" built in no time at all!*

To be sure, lots of things drag on far longer than they should—political campaigns, road construction projects, the TV soap opera *General Hospital*. But some things can't be rushed. Take diamonds and oak trees, for example. Or consider the miracle that is pregnancy. There's no way to expedite that nine-month process.

And so it is with the person who has a depleted soul.

When I first faced the reality that I had knackered myself right into a bad case of pastoral burnout, a Christian counselor told me flatly, "You didn't get this way overnight. You won't get healthy overnight either."

I nodded my most humble nod and mumbled, "You're right."

Internally I thought, *You could not be more wrong! What about the power of prayer? What about God's healing touch? What about all the great books and seminars available? I bet I can YouTube my situation, listen to some podcasts, and be back to my old self in no time!*

About that same time my elder board realized I'd never taken a true sabbatical in 20-plus years of ministry. When they graciously told me to disappear for six weeks, I was tempted to taunt my burnout: *Your days are numbered!*

For 40-plus days, I did my best Rip Van Winkle impersonation. I didn't set an alarm clock. I dozed midmornings and took postlunch naps. I watched movies on Netflix. I pondered the biblical account of the prophet Elijah's burnout (1 Kings 16–19). I read several profound books about the soul, wearing out a couple of highlighters in the process. I journaled, took walks, and went to counseling. I even spent time at the lake house of some generous friends, gawking at God's gorgeous creation. It was six weeks of very little *doing* and a whole lot of *being*.

Would you believe that when I got to the end, I felt *more* tired than I had when I started?

Medical experts helped me see that when workaholics push too hard and for too long without resting, their bodies start pumping adrenaline just to keep up. The problem is our adrenal glands were designed to provide only an occasional, short-term boost—mostly for emergencies. Adrenaline was never meant to power our lives in an ongoing way. Embracing a restless lifestyle long term, then, wreaks havoc on our bodies, souls, minds, and spirits. We don't realize just how depleted we really are until we finally stop. At that point we may as well assume the crash position.

Now, to be sure, after the inevitable crash, prayer and people and prescriptions, truths and books, can help us recover. But when we get to the place of sheer exhaustion, what we need more than anything else is time.

Think about it. It's possible to refill a glass of water in a couple of seconds. Refilling a pond can take weeks, even months. What about something as big as a soul? "You may need a year or more," my counselor warned. He was right.

Why God works this way is a great mystery. In some Bible stories, he works so quickly. One word, one touch, and grim situations are instantly reversed, lives are immediately restored. What we often gloss over in the pages of Scripture is how, more often than not, God takes his dear, sweet time. He delays and defers. Sometimes—I can't lie—it almost seems like he dawdles.

How else do we explain those long stretches in biblical history when the people of God were just "waiting on the Lord"? Every time we turn a page, it's 40 years of this hard situation or 400 years of that unresolved mess.

Make no mistake: God *always* does what he promises. But, clearly, he's in no rush to get around to it. Quick fixes are the exception, not the rule. For most of the Bible, big chunks of seemingly uneventful time are front and center.

If you're seriously depleted from a crisis or tragedy or from pushing too hard for too long, you're going to need to embrace a crucial truth: Time is a primary, necessary component of your restoration. Time isn't your enemy; it's your friend. You need to see the long, slow journey to wholeness as every bit as important as the destination. And there's no sense in trying to speed things along, because God is *not* in a hurry. You will get there when he says you will and not one day sooner.

Is there a hack here? Yes. A two-parter…

First, be patient with God. Though his purposes and processes are tedious, they're also transformative. While you are rolling your eyes and tapping your foot waiting, he's doing far more than you imagine. He's using the chisel of time to shape you in deep ways you can't yet see.

Second, be patient with yourself. Fight that powerful urge to try to speed up the healing process. Hurry is the dysfunctional response of a disordered and deluded heart. It's a big part of what got you in trouble in the first place! Trust me, racing to try to get well is like gulping seawater to quench your thirst. It will backfire on you big time.

One day I heard a thump on our glass patio door. Walking over to investigate, I saw a beautiful ruby-throated hummingbird lying still on the brick pavers.

I winced. Everyone knows that hummingbirds have only two speeds: frenetic and dead. This little guy's whizzing and buzzing days were clearly over, brought to a screeching halt by an unyielding pane of glass.

Only they weren't over.

After a few seconds, the bird moved slightly, and then he struggled to get into an upright position. There he sat, very still. He looked so groggy that you could almost see the little cartoon stars swirling above his head. I left. When I returned a couple of hours later to check on him, he was gone.

After a big crash, it takes a while to regain your bearings. So here's permission to sit and recharge. Take as much time as you need.

# WHEN THE IDEA OF REPENTING LEAVES YOU COLD

Quick—name a word in the English language that could use an image consultant more than the word *repent*.

Ha-ha-ha. Trick question. There isn't one. No word is in greater need of a makeover.

Disagree? Think I'm exaggerating? Try this at your next social gathering: As you work the room, drop the word *repent* into your conversations and note the reactions. At least one person will cringe—guaranteed. Watch people stiffen, perhaps even leave the room. By the third and fourth mentions, you'll see a head shake here, a jaw clench there. You'll observe people's eyes doing all sorts of crazy things—flashing or widening or rolling—and that's if you're in a *religious* crowd. (In other circles you're likely to see and hear far worse.)

When it comes to the word *repent*, nobody is neutral, and most folks are negative. Maybe you hear it and are triggered too.

Why? Is it because *repent* is most often found on the lips of angry people who like to yell at "sinners"? Is it because people sometimes spray-paint the word on overpasses[1] as though it were some sort of religious curse word? What are we not seeing in the six letters and two syllables[2] of this old Bible word?

Last question: Is it possible that repenting might be a hack for improving our lives?

Let's start with a little research. The Old Testament word translated *repent* is the Hebrew בוש (shub). This common verb means "to turn around or return; to go back." Picture someone going in one direction and then doing a 180, and you've got it.

In the New Testament, *repent* is a translation of the Greek word μετανοέω (metanoeo), which literally means "to change the mind." In other words, people, upon receiving vital information, humbly and wisely adjust their lives accordingly.

When we put these ideas together (change your mind + turn around), *repent* takes on a whole new connotation. Even though some people use it—regrettably—as an angry denunciation, that's not the idea at all. The word *repent* is a gracious invitation to rethink and redirect one's life. How about that? Repenting has nothing to do with being verbally humiliated and everything to do with being smart. It's getting needed input and making a basic course correction.

Does repenting involve emotion? It might or it might not, but it *always* involves action. James I. Packer put it this way: "Repentance, as we know, is basically not moaning and remorse, but turning and change."

Is repenting always religious in nature? No. When your doctor warns you to modify your diet and start exercising or risk becoming diabetic, she's essentially telling you to *repent* without using the word. And she's not trying to shame you; she's trying to help you.

Same with the business-savvy friend who emails you a couple of old news articles and somberly urges you to read up on an entrepreneur's track record before you invest your hard-earned savings in the guy's new start-up.

When Jesus began his public ministry, he had a simple message: "The Kingdom of God is near! Repent of your sins and believe the Good News!" (Mark 1:15 NLT). Here's why that's significant. If Mark's Gospel is the earliest of the four Gospels (as many scholars believe), then this command to repent is the first recorded command of Jesus.

Notice that in encouraging people to repent, Jesus was announcing "Good News." (Question: How does one do that without a grin?) Christ was essentially saying. "Wake up! Open your eyes! You don't have to keep living in the same old ways. Trust me and all that I'm telling you!"

Repent and believe...this was Jesus's summary for how to *begin* a relationship with God. According to the rest of the New Testament, it's also the blueprint for what it looks like to *continue* a relationship with God. We're called to a lifestyle of continually turning back and trusting. As John Calvin pointed out, "Repentance is not merely the start of the Christian life; it is the Christian life." Author A.W. Pink gave this sober warning: "The Christian who has stopped repenting has stopped growing."

Most Christians are comfortable talking about faith. I'm guessing you've been in circles where friends shared openly about how they were trusting God for this or that. People have probably encouraged you to "keep the faith" and "live by faith" and "fight the good fight of faith."

How do we get better at discussing repentance? Imagine sitting in a circle where people are talking honestly and nonjudgmentally about the places in their lives where they're asking God for help to turn around. Could that happen?

It could. And it needs to. We need circles of belief *and* repentance. But before we'll ever have *groups* like that, we need *individual* Christians who are good repenters.

As we've already seen, the first step in becoming a good repenter is to repent of one's bogus ideas about repentance! The widely accepted idea that repenting means wearing a dunce cap in the corner of the sanctuary and sobbing while everyone else points scornfully at you needs to go. It's a lie. Repentance isn't shameful; it's smart. It's receiving gracious insight from above and letting the truth change our thinking again and again so we're continuously turning back to God and trusting him once more.

Want a good hack? The next time you pick up a Bible, pray something like this: "Lord, you've called me to follow you in a life of repentance and faith. Now, as I open and read your Word, show me what I need to turn *from*. Then grant me the grace to return to you in ever deepening trust."

The next time a friend asks, "How can I pray for you?" how about answering, "Pray I'll get better and better at repenting."

11

# WHEN YOU NEED TO PRAY BUT YOU'RE ALL OUT OF WORDS

Have you ever experienced writer's block? You sit at your computer, and the keys are *right there*. But finding words is like finding Sasquatch in the Pacific Northwest or missing jets in the Bermuda Triangle.

Good luck.

I've been afflicted. Trust me, when the words won't come, the fingers can't move. And when the keys aren't pushed, the screen remains blank. Thankfully, my worst case of writer's block lasted only a few days. I know some writers who have been blocked for *months*.

Far worse than writer's block—and much more universal—is "pray-er's" block. I wonder if you've faced this dilemma. (Perhaps you have a case of it right now.) You want to pray—you desperately *need* to pour out your soul to God—but you can't find the words.

Sometimes this happens because we're physically exhausted or emotionally spent. The mere thought of forming coherent thoughts and voicing them to God feels like climbing Everest. Other times we're wordless in prayer because we're confused. Life events are coming at us so rapidly and from so many directions at once that we don't know what to think, much less what to say.

During one especially chaotic season in my life, I told a friend, "Every day it's like I'm holding on for dear life to a log that's being swept down a raging, rocky river. I'm utterly out of control, barely keeping my head above the waterline, trying somehow to survive the next patch of rapids."

Ever feel like that? If so, you know that during such times, you're not exactly sitting around composing eloquent petitions to God.

What do we do when we need to pray but for whatever reason we can't summon the words?

Let me share two encouraging reminders and one ingenious hack.

First, the reminders.

The Bible assures Christians that the resurrected Jesus "is able to save completely those who come to God through him, *because he always lives to intercede for them*" (Hebrews 7:25, emphasis added; see also Romans 8:34 and 1 John 2:1). Reread Hebrews 7:25 slowly. It's telling you something astounding: Jesus is continually praying for you. He is praying for you *at this very moment* and in all those times you can't muster any words to pray!

That's not all. It gets even better. The apostle Paul writes of the Holy Spirit, "If we don't know how or what to pray, it doesn't matter.

He does our praying in and for us, making prayer out of our wordless sighs, our aching groans" (Romans 8:26 MSG).

During the stressful period of my life I just mentioned, I did a lot of wordless sighing and achy groaning. Then one day I heard myself whisper the prayer, "Please, God…"

The end. No other words followed—not even the customary "Amen." "Please, God…" was all I had.

Later, I caught myself muttering the phrase again…and again. Before long, I realized I was unconsciously repeating this two-word plea throughout my waking hours! The prayer was involuntary. Automatic. I'm convinced it was exactly what Paul talked about in Romans 8—a Spirit-prompted, Spirit-guided groan from the depths of a heart too confused and weary to utter anything more.

But what did it mean? Sometimes I think my sighing was shorthand for, "Give me the strength to take another step." On other occasions it meant, "Give me peace amid all this chaos." "Please, God…" "Please, God…" It was natural and unforced, a perfect, all-occasion prayer.

In that season of ten thousand "Please, God" prayers, I was coming face-to-face with the same truth that the great John Bunyan once discovered: "In prayer it is better to have a heart without words than words without a heart."

I was also unknowingly engaging in an ancient spiritual practice (or hack, if you will). Some in the Eastern church would call my prayers "breath prayers" or "prayers of the heart."

What's a breath prayer? It's a short petition to God from the depths of one's soul, expressed over and over rhythmically, like breathing. In breath prayer, it's as though we're exhaling stress or fear or unbelief and inhaling the reality that God is near and good.

Breath prayer is how some Christians attempt to carry out the biblical command to "pray continually" (1 Thessalonians 5:17).

The most famous breath prayer is the "Jesus Prayer": "Lord Jesus Christ, Son of God, have mercy on me, a sinner."[1] While breathing in, a practitioner prays the first half of that sentence—"Lord Jesus Christ, Son of God…" Then, while exhaling, he or she prays the remainder of the short petition—"have mercy on me, a sinner." The goal, as in all spiritual practices (or hacks), isn't mindless repetition; it's mindful recognition. It's a way of remembering, *God is with me, and I want to orient my heart toward him and live consciously in his presence.*[2]

Breath prayer is perfect for overwhelmed believers and wordless saints. When we're struggling to express all that's taking place in our hearts and lives, the Bible provides countless, short phrases we can whisper back to God.

An utterance I've used often in times of lagging faith is based on Mark 9:24: "Lord, I do believe…help my unbelief." When I need reminders of God's faithful love, I sometimes whisper, "Your love, O Lord…endures forever" (from Psalm 136). When I'm weary, a helpful breath prayer is, "My soul finds rest…in God alone" (from Psalm 62:1). When I'm fearful, I can repeat the reminder from Psalm 56:3, "When I am afraid…I put my trust in you." A recent favorite is, "Make your home, O Christ…in my heart through faith" (from Ephesians 3:17).

If you have plenty of words, fantastic! Go ahead and pray long, eloquent prayers. Just don't ever buy into the lie that God prefers big, wordy prayers over terse, heartfelt cries like "Please, God…"

## 12

# WHEN YOUR DEVOTIONAL LIFE IS STALE AND BLAH

As I mentioned earlier, during my first semester at college, I went on a religious retreat with about 250 other students. Lest you're tempted to think of me more highly than you ought, let me confess: I did not go on this weekend getaway because I was hungering and thirsting for righteousness. I went to meet girls.

Sad, but true. Thankfully, God's grace superseded my less-than-honorable motives. At a long-gone campground called Camp Atakapa, I heard a speaker named Dan Hayes talk about a moment-by-moment relationship with Christ. The longer he spoke, the more I felt my restless heart pulse with hope. *Yes!* I thought. *That! Sign me up for that!*

Immediately, I was filled with questions about God, Jesus, the Bible, and more. Noting my wild-eyed spiritual curiosity (and, I'm sure, hoping to point me in a healthy direction), an upperclassman named Clayton Hays took me under his wing. He first made sure I understood the meaning of the gospel—that is, the good news of Jesus's life, death, and resurrection. Then he showed me how to have an appointment with God (what lots of Christians call a "devotional time" or a "quiet time").

"Don't overthink it," my older, wiser friend said. "All we're talking about is a focused conversation with God, ten to twenty minutes every day, ideally in the morning. The conversation involves two parts: Listening to God speak to you through the words of the Bible and then talking back to him via prayer. You read a section from the Bible, and then you respond to God by telling him whatever's on your heart and asking him to live in and through you."

Would you believe this simple practice immediately became the highlight of my life? No kidding. Every night for at least a couple of months, I was like a kid on Christmas Eve, too keyed-up to sleep because of what awaited me in the morning! Having a devotional/prayer time was awesome!

Until it wasn't.

I don't know exactly when the thrill wore off, but surely by the holidays I noticed that "spending time with God" was about as exciting as doing my laundry. Some days I got unbelievably quiet during my quiet time—as in, I fell asleep. The times I didn't doze off, I'd sit there thinking, *What am I doing wrong?* Too bad nobody shared with me Frank Laubach's wise words: "If you are weary of some sleepy form of devotion, probably God is as weary of it as you are."

Turns out I wasn't doing anything wrong. In his classic book *The Screwtape Letters,* C.S. Lewis writes about the normal phenomenon I was experiencing. Often, he suggests, when people begin a relationship with Christ—or have an episode of renewed faith—they experience a surge of emotion and spiritual enthusiasm. It's very much like falling in love. The heart swells with warm, tender feelings toward God, and the mind has a challenging time focusing on anything else. During such times we don't think of spiritual pursuits as duties. On the contrary, we find ourselves filled with desire to be with God—a kind of holy longing. Drawing near to God in worship or prayer or by reading the Bible is a delight, not drudgery.

However, Lewis notes, God inevitably "withdraws, if not in fact, (then) at least from…conscious experience…He leaves the creature to stand up on its own legs—to carry out from the will alone duties which have lost all relish."[1]

In other words, waning passions are part of the normal spiritual growth process. Consider this: If knowing Christ meant a thrill-a-minute life of nonstop goose bumps, why would we ever need faith?

In those seasons when your devotional life feels drab and lackluster, you don't need spiritual fireworks (and you sure don't need to stop having devotions!). What you need is a creative hack, a devotional change of pace.

Here are three practical ways to breathe new life into your time with God.

1. *Change your expectations.* Remember that the goal of a devotional time isn't to read *x* number of Bible verses or to pray for a certain number of minutes. Nor is the point to get emotionally fired up. The goal is simply to be with God. With that in mind, the next time you meet with God, don't read, write, or say a word. Merely sit quietly for ten or fifteen minutes in absolute silence. Your only goal? To be present to God. Do that, and then whether you *feel* anything or not, that's a great devotional time!

2. *Change your scenery.* On a practical level, if you normally sit inside, take your Bible out to the deck, patio, or porch. Even better, go for a "walk and talk" with God around the neighborhood, or grab your car keys and drive to a local park, or find an open church building and bask in the stillness of the sanctuary.

3. *Change your routine.*

- If you usually read the Bible and pray at bedtime, be like Jesus and get up while it's still dark (Mark 1:35). Go outside and listen to the world wake up. Consider how big and good God is. Think about how near he is (even if you can't sense his nearness).

- Devote your entire time alone with God to streaming a few hymns or praise songs on your computer or phone. Sing them softly to God (or loudly if you're alone or you have a voice like Adele or Ed Sheeran).

- Try reading from a different Bible translation (or a modern paraphrase of the Bible).

- Instead of reading the Bible and *then* praying, do both at once. Pray the Word *of* God *to* God. For example, adapt a psalm to your life situation and pray it back to God. Or make Paul's beautiful prayers for the Ephesians in chapters 1 and 3 your own.

- How about this? Turn to a story in the Gospels—for example, the story about Jesus and his disciples in the boat during the storm (Matthew 8:23-27; Mark 4:35-41; or Luke 8:22-25). But don't simply *read* it; *live* it! Put yourself in the story, in the boat, and in the storm. Close your eyes. Can you smell the seawater? Can you feel the fear that's growing in the disciples' hearts as the wind picks up and the waves get higher? Now watch Peter and the others nudge Jesus awake. Pay close attention to what Christ does. Listen attentively to his words. Notice what this whole experience does in and to your heart.

- If you don't normally do so, try journaling your honest thoughts, feelings, fears, and prayers. You'll be amazed at the deep things that surface when you give yourself permission to write out—unedited—whatever's swirling in your soul. If you're worried about someone finding your confessions and secrets, type them into a password-protected file on your computer.

- Choose a short verse of Scripture and spend ten minutes memorizing it. (Read it repeatedly. Say it again and again until you can write it out by heart.) Then mull it over for another ten minutes. Consider its implications—what it says about God, about you, about the situations you're facing.

If, as the old saying goes, variety is the spice of life, then surely a little devotional variety can spice up your spiritual life. Want to wake up your time with God? Throw it a curveball.

## 13

# WHEN YOU'RE FEELING BIG PRESSURE TO RESCUE SOMEONE

The caller's name was Donnie Bryant. He was in serious trouble, he said, because not a single Christian had been willing to help him. And now, he said, he was going to kill himself by jumping off a bridge.

My heart stopped beating momentarily...and then started racing wildly. I was a wet-behind-the-ears, 21-year-old rookie youth pastor. No one had ever briefed me on situations like this.

The desperate caller spouted Bible verses about loving one's neighbor. He ranted about hypocrisy in the church. The longer he talked, the guiltier and more responsible I felt. *What if I do nothing and this guy does a swan dive into the mighty Mississippi? Lord, show me what to do! Help me save him!*

It never occurred to me that even as I was silently praying for this man, he was shrewdly preying on me. Donnie Bryant had found an easy mark.

I'm mortified to admit this next part, but in less than one hour, this smooth-talking stranger had convinced me to 1) meet him in the lobby of one of Baton Rouge's fanciest hotels[1] and 2) drive him to my bank and withdraw $300 cash to briefly "loan" him.

As I dropped him back at the swanky hotel, he smiled. (Come to think of it in hindsight, it was kind of a Grinch-y smile.) I was the first Christian to ever trust him, he said. If I returned in three hours, he'd repay me every cent, he said.

I shake my head as I recount these embarrassing details. Do I really need to tell you how the story ends?

On second thought, I just did.

Something in human nature loves to play the hero. We don't merely want to save face or save our own skin; we want to save the day, save the damsel in distress, save the world. We'll try to rescue almost anything—abandoned dogs, beached whales, a deal that's going south, old houses and cars—even a toxic dating relationship that needs to be put out of its (and our) misery.

I think this is why we line up to watch *Ironman* and *Wonder Woman*. It's why most guys secretly or not so secretly wish they were Jason Bourne or Ethan Hunt. At its best (think scuba divers who rescue a Taiwanese boys' soccer team trapped in an underwater cave), this trait is a glorious reminder that we are made in the image of a compassionate God who comes to seek and save the perishing. At its worst, this desire becomes warped and disfigured. We aren't content to play the assigned part of caretaker or caregiver. We want the starring role of Savior (with a capital *S*).

This greed for ultimate glory goes all the way back to Eden—to humanity's primal desire to be like God. It wasn't enough that God gave Adam and Eve important tasks to perform. Staring at the

Tree of the Knowledge of Good and Evil in the middle of the garden, they concluded, "There's our ticket. Once we eat from that tree, we'll know everything God knows. We'll have no need to look up for salvation; we'll be able to look within and save ourselves. And we'll also be able to look around and save anyone else who happens to get in trouble."

Some people have this *savior syndrome* worse than others. Here's a little test to see how badly you're affected:

\_\_\_\_ You let con artists misuse the Bible to guilt you into giving them $300.[2]

\_\_\_\_ You constantly find yourself drawn to people who are emotional black holes and Grand Canyons of neediness.

\_\_\_\_ It nearly kills you to say no or "I'm sorry, I can't" to a request for help (even when you're already stressed to the breaking point).

\_\_\_\_ You engage in long arguments with coworkers (or strangers online)—even when it's obvious they don't buy into your religious beliefs or political opinions.

\_\_\_\_ You typically resort to *whatever it takes*—even guilt, shame, manipulation, coercion, or electing demagogues—to get people to do what you're convinced they need to do.

\_\_\_\_ You keep trying to change your spouse—even though all such attempts have been unsuccessful, unwanted, and the source of much unhappiness for your entire marriage.

_____ You routinely bail out your children when they act irresponsibly.

_____ You try to protect your friends or group members from the consequences of their bad choices—and you decide it's your fault when they make wrong decisions.

Even two check marks are too much. Three to five? I'm guessing you're tired, stressed, and frustrated most of your waking hours. Six to eight? All you need is a cape and an agent and you're ready to star in your own Marvel superhero series.

Two things are true: 1) It's terrible to see people in pain or danger, and 2) it's terrific to want to see them whole and safe. However, it's not our job to play God. That role's too big for us. We can't pull it off. While our bumbling efforts to rescue people (usually involving some kind of carrot-and-stick approach) can sometimes result in short-term behavior modification, only the Almighty has the wisdom and power to truly fix people. He alone can bring about deep healing and lasting transformation of the heart.

What, then, is the hack when we realize we've tried to usurp God's role in the great unfolding drama of life?

It's to reread "the script" and resume playing the role we've been given.

Again, that role isn't "Savior" (Someone more gifted has that part). We're supporting actors. Every day, if we're paying attention, we're being directed to *love*, not save, family members and friends, neighbors and strangers. Our part is to draw near them and open our hearts and lives—and in some, but not all, situations, our wallets. Our role is to engage, ask questions, listen compassionately, pray fervently, and show and tell the gospel. Sometimes we'll be given opportunities to do a little Spirit-guided improvisation such as speaking truth, challenging wrong thinking, or passing along hard-earned wisdom on the fly.

Mostly, however, our role is to point hurting folks to the One who really *can* rescue them.

I pray somebody is doing that for Donnie Bryant today. Or how cool would it be if, after all these years, he's now doing that for others?

# 14

# WHEN YOUR FAITH IS OVERDUE FOR A CHECKUP

Nobody I know likes routine medical checkups. I suspect this is because checkups involve a host of intrusive questions.

- The doctor: "How about we step up on the scales here and get our weight?"[1]

- The financial adviser: "How's it going with the budget and savings plan we agreed on last January?"

- The dentist: "Have you been flossing regularly?"[2]

- The mechanic: "Did you know your cylinder head is cracked?"

    "I did not. Think it'd be okay to wait a few months to fix that?"

    "Depends. What kind of roadside assistance plan do you have?"

No, nobody likes checkups, which is why so many people didn't (or don't) love school. School is the Checkup That Keeps Going and Never Stops—day after week after month after year.

Sometimes school checkups come in the form of oral questioning. (Remember class discussions? Remember ducking down behind the student sitting in front of you—the football player with the broad shoulders or the cheerleader with the big hair? Remember praying that the teacher wouldn't see you, call on you, and humiliate you in front of your peers?)

More often, school checkups come in written form: a pop quiz in Spanish vocabulary, a multiple-choice exam in biology, a short-answer test in American Literature. In other classes, the questions are only implied, but we're forced to answer them anyway. How many push-ups can you do in a minute? Can you give a five-minute persuasive speech that is clear and compelling?

Why are academic types so obsessed with questions? They would probably answer that question with another question: How better to assess where a student is in the learning process? Questions show how much someone is grasping and internalizing. What's more, good questions, used skillfully, can motivate students to go even higher and further.

A few years ago, I began noticing how many questions Jesus asked during his brief ministry.[3] Everywhere I turned in the Gospels, I found him giving his students (his disciples) another oral exam. (In some instances, he even quizzed his inquisitors!)

I noticed something else. The questions Jesus asked weren't

conversational fluff. They were in-your-face, grab-you-by-the-throat inquiries.

Seeing that, I then noticed a third thing. Whenever I came to an especially pointed question of Jesus, I tried to sneak past it. I'd act as if it didn't pertain to me and then start looking frantically for a nearby verse to duck behind! Bottom line? I didn't want Jesus poking around in my heart. I mean, it's one thing to find out you have high cholesterol; it's a different matter altogether to realize your very soul is a twisted mess.

Over time, I noticed a fourth reality about the questions of Jesus. They are living and active (Hebrews 4:12). You might be able to tune them out for a time, but you can't elude them forever. They will chase you. Eventually, they will run you down and pin your skittish soul to the ground.

It took a while, but I finally cried, "Uncle!" I surrendered to the truth that *spiritual* checkups (like all other kinds of checkups) are good—even if they're not exactly fun. As a result, I reread the Gospels carefully and typed up 31 of Jesus's most penetrating questions—one for each day of the month. Then I started letting the Lord quiz me on a regular basis.

Here's just part of my list—enough to get you started on this helpful hack.

1. "Who do you say that I am?" (Mark 8:29 NASB)

2. "What do you benefit if you gain the whole world but lose your own soul? Is anything worth more than your soul?" (Matthew 16:26 NLT)

3. "Do you love me?" (John 21:16)

4. "Do you want to get well?" (John 5:6)

5. "Where is your faith?" (Luke 8:25 ESV)

6. "Why do you keep calling me 'Lord, Lord!' when you don't do what I say?" (Luke 6:46 NLT)

7. "You of little faith, why are you so afraid?" (Matthew 8:26)

8. "Why do you see the speck that is in your brother's eye, but do not notice the log that is in your own eye?" (Matthew 7:3 ESV)

9. "Why are you sleeping?" (Luke 22:46)

10. "Why does this generation ask for a sign?" (Mark 8:12)

11. "If I am telling the truth, why don't you believe me?" (John 8:46)

12. "Can all your worries add a single moment to your life?" (Matthew 6:27 NLT)

13. "Will you really lay down your life for me?" (John 13:38)

14. "What do you want me to do for you?" (Matthew 20:32 NASB)

Here's my challenge. Each day for the next two weeks, sit attentively with one of these questions of Jesus. Read it carefully—in its context (the chapter/passage in which it's found). Then mull it over prayerfully. Answer it honestly and discuss your answer with Jesus. Then watch what happens in your life.

Unless you're dead, pondering these 14 questions (and all the others Jesus asks) will be like wrestling with a defibrillator. Sometimes I read my daily question and feel a strong urge to plead the Fifth Amendment! An *honest* answer would be too incriminating and reveal what a monumental mess my heart is. But although these questions make me squirm, they also comfort me. If the truth in the question undresses me, the grace in the Questioner covers me. (If I were into tattoos, maybe these questions would be perfect for the inside of my eyelids.)

Who would have imagined that a spiritual checkup could be such a blessed thing? What initially feels like an interrogation is in truth the necessary first step in our transformation.

# WHEN YOUR HEART IS FULL (BUT NOT IN THE BEST OF WAYS OR WITH THE BEST OF THINGS)

t happens on a semiregular basis. You're scrolling through your feed on social media when you come across a picture that's not just pretty; it's piercing. You gasp. This is the way you imagine Eden must have looked, when the world was as it should be, before the "Great Calamity" plunged everything into sadness.

Maybe the picture is of a wedding party in a candlelit meadow at sunset. They're dancing joyously, indifferent to the camera, oblivious to everything but the indescribable happiness of the moment. A few days later it's a different, yet similar photo—a sleeping, smiling newborn in the big, strong arms of her dozing dad.

The caption on both posts is the same and says it all: "My heart is full!"

Can we go ahead and admit the obvious? Nothing beats a full heart.

I think of how all the people I meet are full of assorted things. Some are full of the devil, and I confess that far too many days, I'm full of *myself*, which isn't much better. Just like you, I know plenty of folks full of hot air, bologna, or malarkey (and without a doubt, some of them think this of us). I smile at younger friends who are full of spit and vinegar—which is to say, they're full of energy and mischief as well as promise. I talk often with older souls who are full of regret.

"My heart is full!" is usually an exclamation of joy. But it can also be a cry for help. I'm referring to those times my heart feels uncomfortably stuffed and rumbly—the way your stomach can feel after a cross-country road trip.

You know that awful feeling. After two weeks and three thousand miles of bored snacking—and ingesting fast food from the three basic food groups: greasy, sweet, and salty—you feel bloated and queasy. (Why do they call it comfort food when it leaves you so uncomfortable?)

Now you just want to eat something healthy: fresh blueberries, or even—you never thought you'd hear yourself say this—a plate of kale. *Anything* that hasn't been deep fried and dusted with sugar.

Spiritually speaking, our hearts can get like that and feel like that. They're full all right, but of all the wrong things.

What then? What's the remedy for indigestion of the soul?

I've been using a food metaphor—no point in switching now. Sometimes I imagine my heart as a filled bowl. (To help, I'll even sit with my hands cupped together in my lap.[1]) Then I prayerfully reflect on what exactly is gurgling around in my heart and making me feel so spiritually nauseated. In effect, I pray, *God, show me what I'm full of.*

Almost always it's a cornucopia of unhealthy junk. One day, I realize my soul is swollen with fear, anger, worry, discontent, or envy. Another day, I find my heart is overflowing with unbelief and pride. Sometimes I notice I'm stuffed with all sorts of ugly attitudes—I'm critical and judgmental, ungrateful, pessimistic about the future, or harboring a grudge.

Honestly? This part of the hack is no fun. But what happens next is where it gets good.

I picture all that junk filling my heart (imagining it there in my cupped hands), and then *I dump it out!* I literally tip my hands as if I were dumping out the contents of a bowl onto the floor. As I do, I confess, praying something like, *God, I'm sick—almost literally—of having a heart so full of such things* [typically I name them here, one by one]. *Thank you for the forgiveness you promise to those who admit their need* (1 John 1:19).

Then I symbolically raise my cupped hands (my now-empty bowl or heart, as it were) and ask the Lord to fill it, to fill me. *Christ, make your home in me. Fill me with your Holy Spirit. Fill me with all the fullness of God* (Ephesians 3:17; 5:18; 3:19). I think about all the things I *know* I'll need that day, and I say prayers like, *Lord, give me grace. I sure could use some wisdom. I'm weak. Give me your strength. And peace. How I need your peace today! And, Lord, don't stop there. Fill my heart with kindness, eternal perspective, self-control, a willingness to serve others.*

With my hands still upturned like a bowl, then I pray about specific situations I'm facing:

"Give me a forgiving heart for ____."

"Grant me courage in talking with ____."

"Fill me with joy as I ____."

This quick exercise is reminiscent of what D.L. Moody once

described: "Before we pray that God would fill us, I believe we ought to pray that He would empty us. There must be an emptying before there can be a filling."

Hey, we're going to be full of something, right? Instead of a junk-filled soul that makes people want to run the other direction, why not ask for a God-filled life that makes people pause, gasp, and think about what could be?

# 16

# WHEN YOU'RE TOO WRAPPED UP IN YOUR OWN LIFE

When I was a kid, my Uncle Ollie owned a large printing press—the old kind accompanied by big drawers full of movable lead type. This contraption filled up his garage, and with it he printed all sorts of short essays, poems, and inspiring quotes.

Once he gave me a card titled "The Teen Commandments." I'm not joking. It included ten directives like these:

1. Be honest.

2. Study hard.

3. Don't smoke.

4. Be punctual.

5. Take care of your possessions.

I can't remember the rest.

Even though I was never able to locate this list of requirements in the Bible, they sounded pretty good to me.

Another time, Uncle Ollie gave me a little stack of business cards that read:

**SelfIshNess**

I still have one of those SelfIshNess cards.[1] I have no idea if Uncle Ollie's one-word sermon on card stock affected anyone else, but I know it caused me to ponder: *Hmmm. How about that? Lurking within every act of selfishness is S-I-N. I guess if it weren't for S-I-N, there would be no selfishness.*

I still think about those old cards when I read the story in Genesis 3. For some unknown amount of time prior to listening to the lies of the serpent, Adam and Eve never sinned, never did a single selfish thing. They were so utterly focused on loving God and serving each other that it never even occurred to them that they were naked!

Everything changed the moment they ate the forbidden fruit. Their gazes turned inward. They became painfully self-conscious and sinfully self-protective. Then they started popping out little brats who were just like them—self-absorbed, self-exalting, self-important. They were self-reliant and self-serving offspring whose descendants would eventually buy self-help books by the millions and take selfies by the billions.

Here's the sad and ugly truth: When humanity fell into sin (turned away from God and *jumped* into sin is more like it), selfishness became our default mode. Selfishness is why I instinctively look first *for* myself and *at* myself when I view a group snapshot that includes me. It's why my first response is frustration—not concern for others—when the big game I'm watching is interrupted by a special news or weather report. Selfishness is why I become so immersed in *my* problems, *my* projects, *my* life, *my* bills, *my* kids, *my* this, *my* that… My oh my oh my.

The grim truth? If you and I don't fight to recognize and renounce this natural tendency (and work to replace all our "me" thoughts with "you and them" thoughts), we will spend our fleeting days fixated on our sad selves.

What, then, is the hack? How do we keep our self-centered tendencies from metastasizing into full-blown narcissism?

This surely isn't "the" only hack for that, but it's a good one.

A few days ago, I drove to a coffee shop to meet a guy. Though we'd met at church and become Facebook friends, Brooks and I had never had a meaningful conversation.

We sat down and made some small talk, and then I had a great impulse—God-prompted, I'm convinced. I blurted, "Hey, I don't know anything about your background. Tell me your story."

For the next 30 or so minutes, I was on the edge of my chair. My new friend told me about coming to faith as a child and then losing two older, adopted brothers to suicide. He talked about a lot of "wasted years" during high school, college, and then postcollege. He opened up about a failed marriage and an automobile accident that took both his parents. Mostly, he kept pausing to shake his head in wonder at how God had been so kind and gracious to him, especially during all those years when he was being his most selfish self.

Here's what I noticed: While giving him my full attention, I was delivered from the terrible curse of SelfIshNess for at least half an hour! I was immersed in the sometimes tragic, ultimately glorious story of someone else. Not only that, but I was awakened to the bigger and wilder story God is telling in the world.

I came away *humbled.* Sitting there sipping Rwandan java on a quiet Friday afternoon, I was reminded of that great line that's been attributed to everyone from Plato to Philo to Ian Maclaren: "Be kind, for everyone you meet is fighting a hard battle." Of all the true sayings in this world, that's one of the truest. My friend Walt Wiley expresses it this way: "Behind every face, there's a drama." I left the coffee shop asking myself, *How many struggling souls do I blow past or blow off because I'm so wrapped up in my own life?* And I left there praying, *Lord, help me consider others to be more important than myself* (Philippians 2:3).

I also came away *motivated* to be more intentional about getting face-to-face with others, looking new friends in the eye and saying, "Hey, tell me your story" and looking old friends in the eye and saying, "Hey, tell me the latest chapter in your story."

Finally, I came away *encouraged.* Brooks's story reminded me that God is big and good and doing astonishing things in the world. He's changing lives all around us. But we'll never see those miracles, much less celebrate them, until we lift our heads and look beyond our own situations.

Obsessing over your life? Trapped in SelfIshNess?

Go grab a cup of joe with some Joe or Jo and say, "Tell me your story."

# 17

# WHEN YOU'RE NOT IN A GREAT PLACE (EMOTIONALLY SPEAKING)

I wish you could meet my friend Donna.

She works with victims of domestic violence, a job that features lots of drama and not much pay. No matter. Donna is an adventurous, fun-loving soul. She's a "noticer." She sees little "nothing" things that could grow into special things if only somebody would bump the first domino. Her generous heart and curious mind won't turn off, meaning she's constantly scheming, forever dreaming up new ways to solve chronic problems. She's a "connector"—matching people with resources to people with needs. Her ability to help kids navigate and process life's difficulties is breathtaking. (It's no surprise that her umpteen nieces and nephews *adore* her.) In all her free time (ha-ha) she helps lead a successful support co-op for families with foster children.

Donna is one of those people who is making a difference and having an impact. Not that long ago, however, she was in a different place.

To put it mildly, Donna was a restless mess. She was no more broken than anybody else, just dragging around her own set of monogrammed baggage. She seemed to spend all her waking hours fighting either God or her personal demons of loneliness and purposelessness—some days all of the above. She was tired. Angry. Stuck. Her friends often drove over to the dark, depressing apartment (*cave* is a more accurate word) where she lived *(existed* is a more accurate word) to check on her, and they always came away wide-eyed and wordless. When Donna called to talk to my wife, I'd hold my breath. That wasn't easy to do because they stayed on the phone for a *long* time.

Dr. Karl Menninger was the dean of American psychiatry in the twentieth century. As much as anyone, he championed mental health by helping destigmatize and demystify mental illness. While not rejecting conventional treatments, he was famous—and controversial—for some of his unorthodox ideas. For example, once he was asked what advice he would give to someone who felt a nervous breakdown coming on. His answer stunned his listeners: "Lock up your house, go across the railroad tracks, find someone in need, and do something for them."

On another occasion, he expressed the same idea in different terms: "Love cures people—both the ones who give it and the ones who receive it."

And peace of mind? Menninger believed this rare blessing could be experienced only by those who forget themselves in the service of others.

I don't know what specific events triggered her decision, but a few years back Donna unwittingly took Dr. Menninger's advice. Somehow, amid her deep funk, Donna found the grace to surrender her depressing situation to God. Then she did a version of locking up her house and finding some people in need.

A woman introduced her to a young couple with two boys, a three-year-old and a baby. I won't go into the gory details other than to say this little family was at risk in every way it's possible to be at risk. Donna, in between jobs at the time, befriended them and—along with a lot of other people—tried to help them get on their feet. In time, she "unlocked her house," frequently watching the boys while the struggling parents applied for jobs or met with social workers.

Later, when Child Protective Services stepped in, Donna's baby-sitting became full-time fostering. For at least a year, Donna poured herself into those boys. And then came the day when the parents asked Donna this wrenching question: "Would you consider adopting our sons?"

Donna did. Today the boys are thriving, and she is a different person.

Turns out Menninger was right: Love does have a healing effect. And when we forget ourselves to help others, we can find peace.

Let me be clear: This isn't a hack for depression—as though there were any such thing. (For the record, I have been clinically depressed, gone to counseling, and taken antidepressants.) Do *not* for a moment think I'm saying that the quick way to overcome deep emotional pain or self-destructive thoughts is to go be nice to someone.

Depression is a complex, serious condition that affects its victims in every conceivable way: mentally, emotionally, physically, socially.

If you think you might be spiraling downward, I plead with you to consult a qualified medical or mental health professional. Help *is* available, and there is *no* shame in admitting, "I'm not in a good place" and asking, "Can you help me?"

What I *am* saying here is that *one* important aspect of mental health and happiness is looking outward and seeking to be a blessing to others. And it's not just me—or Karl Menninger—saying this. This is what the Bible teaches from start to finish:

- Those who are kind benefit themselves (Proverbs 11:17).

- A generous person will prosper; whoever refreshes others will be refreshed (Proverbs 11:25).

- What I'm interested in seeing you do is: sharing your food with the hungry, inviting the homeless poor into your homes, putting clothes on the shivering ill-clad, being available to your own families. Do this and the lights will turn on, and your lives will turn around at once (Isaiah 58:6-8 MSG).

- Blessed are the merciful, for they will be shown mercy (Matthew 5:7).

- Give, and it will be given to you (Luke 6:38).

- It is more blessed to give than to receive (Acts 20:35).

My friend Donna would say "Amen!" to all of these verses. She knows firsthand the curative power of love.

# WHEN YOU'RE TIRED OF ALL THE PRETENDING

We're part of a culture that doesn't know what it wants.

On the one hand, we listen to compelling Ted Talks urging us to "Be real! Be authentic! Be vulnerable! Tell the truth about your life. Stop obsessing over what everyone else wants you to be and let your true self be seen. You be you!" It's a tantalizing message. It sounds so pure and simple. Our weary hearts cry, "Yes!" because we know how exhausting inauthenticity can be.

But then, right about the time we click off the old YouTube, we get whacked across the noggin by another message. The gist is something like this: "The idea of building an authentic life is noble, even sweet. But what you really should be building is your *brand*! (Unless, of course, 'authenticity' *is* your brand.) Authenticity *is* a good thing. But image, as everyone knows, is everything. Get too real, and you might cease to be relevant. So put your game face on (and maybe your Spanx). Then go out there and project confidence and strength—never let 'em see you sweat."

This is the culture in which we live. We ache to be real, and we also face immense pressure to put on a persona. It's the recipe for whiplash—and crazy-making. This probably explains why I went on Instagram the other day and posted that completely spontaneous selfie of my wife and me by the ocean. Because I'm all about being authentic, though, I'll tell you it was the eighth picture we took because my hair and smile weren't quite on point the first seven tries. Also, after I applied the "Vivid Warm" filter, I looked far less pasty.

We're not about to fix a confused culture here. And God knows, it isn't possible in a thousand or so words to present a comprehensive plan for how to fight inauthenticity in every part of life. But maybe we can focus on one thing: *being real with God.* And maybe, if we can learn authenticity there, at the heart level, it will bubble up to the surface of our lives.

You would think being an "honest-to-God" person would be a breeze. After all, the Bible declares two stunning truths: 1) God knows everything about us—the embarrassing dirt no one else does, all the selfish stunts we'll pull next week and next year...*everything*, and 2) knowing all this, God loves us—full stop with no asterisks, conditions, or preconditions. (Oh, and his love is a *perfect, permanent* love.)

If anything would ever free us up to be transparent and vulnerable with God, it ought to be those facts, right? If nothing about us will ever shock him, and if none of our sins will cause him to stop loving us, shouldn't we be able to bare our souls to him without fear? Shouldn't we be running to him shamelessly and ceaselessly and joyfully?

Ah, but hiding and covering up are in our genes (Genesis 3:7-9). Not only that, but we live in a world where pretending and posing are rewarded, so we interact with God the way we interact with most people. We're coy. We play games and play dumb. We act as if we don't see the rather large elephant we just rode into the room! (And we tell ourselves God doesn't see it either.) We deny eating the Almighty's cookies even as we're brushing cookie crumbs off our sweaters.

Engaging with God, then, becomes one more relationship where we do that strange rhythmic dance of coming close, shrinking back...drawing near, pulling away. We try to hide our unattractive features and put our best foot forward. We're careful not to divulge too much. Because reality can sometimes get...well, a little too real, we like to mix in a little fantasy.

Here's the hack: Grab your soul by the collar, pull it over into the corner, and insist that it start being gut-level honest with God—right now.

I didn't know talking to your own soul was even possible until a few years ago when I noticed people doing it throughout the psalms. The writer of Psalms 42 and 43 was giving his soul the business ("What's *wrong* with you? Why are you *so* worked up?") before he finally ordered it to "Hope in God!" In Psalm 103, David repeatedly exhorted his soul to "Bless the LORD!" (NASB). The author of Psalm 116, after being rescued from a near-death experience, essentially patted his soul on the back and said, "Take a breath. Because God is good, you can relax again."

If biblical saints can say those sorts of things to their souls, shouldn't we modern-day believers be able to tell ours, "Stop being inauthentic with God, and start telling him the truth about your life."

What a novel idea—telling the truth to the "God *of truth*" (Psalm 31:5; Isaiah 65:16 NASB).

After a lengthy and painful period of refusing to come clean with God—and feeling far from God—David had an epiphany. He realized that what God desires is truth "in the innermost being" (Psalm 51:6 NASB)—or, as Eugene Peterson paraphrases that verse in The Message, "What you're after is truth from the inside out."

David got the message. Near the end of the book of Psalms, he celebrated with these words: "The Lord is near to all who call on him, to all who call on him *in truth*" (Psalm 145:18, emphasis added).

In talking about talking to God, C.S. Lewis once said, "We must lay before him what is in us; not what ought to be in us."[1]

That's the spirit. No pretending or spinning. No more trying futilely to hide what's in our hearts from the One the Bible calls "the knower of hearts."[2] Just honesty and authenticity all the way down to the core.

I'm not going to pretend otherwise. This is a *really* good hack: Demand that your soul start telling God the truth, the whole truth, and nothing but the truth.

# 19

# WHEN YOU'RE NOT SURE WHAT TO SAY

Can it really be true that over the course of a lifetime, the average person speaks 450 *million* words?

That's what studies tell us.[1] And that's not counting all the words we *write* in texts, emails, cards, notes, and letters.

Given our extreme chattiness, I'm surprised a) that we don't hear more about vocal cord replacement surgery,[2] and b) that with so much experience talking, we're not experts at knowing exactly what to say in every situation.

Sadly, we're *not* experts at knowing exactly what to say in every situation. We often bite our lips and leave important things unsaid. Or we go to the other extreme—we open our big yappers wide and let fly all sorts of thoughts we should have kept to ourselves.

What's the hack for those conversational moments when our hearts are scrambling for the right words even as they slosh with all kinds of powerful emotions—fear or pride, anger or love, insecurity or gratitude?

The 2007 movie *The Bucket List* is the story of two very different strangers who meet in a cancer ward and decide to try to accomplish a few unfulfilled wishes before they "kick the bucket." Their quest results in some wild adventures, but even more importantly, in some much-needed conversations with loved ones. Driving home the film's central message about living with no regrets is the song "Say" by John Mayer.

Here's all you need to know about that hit tune: Over and over, it urges us to say the things we most *need* to say.

Turns out this simple practice is a helpful hack for all of our human interactions.

Sometimes what we need to say is nothing. Nada. Zero. Zilch. We need to zip our lips. When someone is grieving, for example, they need support, not a platter of homemade platitudes.

My father died when I was in the eleventh grade. I'll never forget my friends Tim and Bill checking out of school and coming over. I don't think they said a dozen words between them. That was fine by me. Their mere presence spoke volumes.

Similarly, an angry spouse (or customer or coworker) needs you to listen, not defend yourself. Besides, if you power up and meet anger with anger, you're likely to deliver the best speech you'll ever regret.

I'm learning that it's a waste of time and verbiage to talk to people who aren't ready to listen. Also, that it's impossible to unsay things. I'm coming to see that the times I keep my big piehole shut, I never make dumb or hurtful or inflammatory comments! Trust me, *nothing* is often the best thing we can say in a situation. Crazy, but true!

On the other hand, sometimes words desperately need to be said—like when there's obvious, unresolved conflict. In such instances, our faith compels us to acknowledge and address the tension. The path to peace often begins with the simple question, "Can we talk?" (Romans 12:18). Then, before sitting down face-to-face to iron out our differences,[3] it's good to say something *to God*: "Jesus, you're the Prince of peace, and you call your followers to be peacemakers. Bless my efforts now. Let your Spirit control and animate me and fill me with peace" (Matthew 5:9; Galatians 5:22-23).

Then, when that hard conversation takes place, what sorts of things do we need to say?

"Here's what I contributed to the situation."

"I was wrong when I ___."

"I'm so sorry I hurt you. Will you please forgive me?"

What about everyday, nonconflict conversations with friends, coworkers, or family members? In those situations, what does it look like to say what we need to say? The Bible records the apostle Paul's words to the Ephesian Christians on this subject. We are to refrain from speaking "unwholesome" words (Ephesians 4:29).[4] Instead, we are to limit our speech to "only what is helpful for building others up according to their needs, that it may benefit those who listen."

The idea here is that what we need to say is *what others need to hear*. We need to ask ourselves—or better yet, ask God—*What verbal encouragement does she need? How can I build him up rather than tear him down?*

Without nagging or being preachy or trite, we can build up others in lots of verbal ways. We can say things like,

"Thank you for ____."
Or a simple "I love you."
How about, "I appreciate you so much" or "What I admire about you is ____"?
Or "I don't say this enough, but I'm *so* proud of you."

When people are struggling, we can say things like,

"I believe in you. You can do this."
"I'm in your corner. I pray for you all the time" (but only if we do, of course).
"Keep fighting the good fight."

Sometimes saying what you need to say means having the courage to say what's uncomfortable when you'd rather clam up and look the other way. Like, for example, after much prayer, saying, "Hey, I've noticed ____, and I'm concerned for you." On those occasions, rather than biting our tongues, we're called to do what the parents of toddlers often say: "Use your words."

Two verses serve as guardrails for me in such moments. I often pray them silently just before—and often *during*—every tough conversation!

> Set a guard, O LORD, over my mouth; keep watch over the door of my lips! (Psalm 141:3 ESV).

> May the words of my mouth and the meditation of my heart be pleasing to you, O LORD, my rock and my redeemer (Psalm 19:14 NLT).

The hack when you're not sure what to say? Say the things you *need* to say.

## 20

# WHEN YOU COULD STAND TO BE MORE THANKFUL

I n a world full of sadness, why should we be thankful? Let us count the ways!

1. *Thankfulness makes us happier.* We know this by experience. When we grouse and gripe our way through a day, focusing on everything that's wrong, we feel rotten by day's end. But when—to use a cheesy cliché—we embrace an attitude of gratitude, our overall mood improves. Did you know our English word *grateful* is related to the old Latin word *gratis*, which means "for nothing, freely"? The point being that grateful people don't have a sense of entitlement. They see life and all its blessings as pure grace—undeserved, delightful gifts. Who has time to complain when there's so much good in which to revel?

2. *Thankfulness makes us more pleasant to be around.* Author Elizabeth Gilbert tells a story about her great-aunt Lolly, whom she calls "a walking exclamation point." When Aunt Lolly received a grim medical diagnosis at age 85, she broke the news to her niece this way: "Hey, Lizard, guess what I have? Cancer. Isn't that interesting?"[1]

How can you not love people like Aunt Lolly? She's what I call a "Grateful," a person who exudes a kind of happy optimism. Gratefuls are the opposite of grim—they're full of wonder and whimsy. They don't bring down the room when they walk in the door. On the contrary, people are glad to see them come and sad to see them go! Gratefuls are 24/7 advertisements for the truth that life is good.

3. *Thankfulness makes us healthier.* Researchers are finding all kinds of correlations between thankfulness and physical health. Gratefuls tend to have lower blood pressure, better sleep patterns, healthier heart rhythms, improved immune function, and a lower incidence of depression. Clinical studies even show that people who keep a "gratitude" journal tend to eat less dietary fat and have decreased cortisol levels (cortisol is a hormone our bodies release when they're stressed).

Why be thankful? So far, we have quite a list: You'll feel better about your life. You'll be more attractive to others. You'll enjoy better health. But there's another reason: *Thankfulness has immense spiritual benefits.*

During his second missionary journey, the apostle Paul started a church in the ancient city of Thessalonica, Greece. A few months later, these new believers sent Paul (who was by that time in Corinth) a list of spiritual questions. His warm reply was what we now know as the First Epistle to the Thessalonians. Tucked away at the end of that letter is an exhortation to cultivate a grateful spirit: "Be thankful in all circumstances, for this is God's will for you who belong to Christ Jesus" (1 Thessalonians 5:18 NLT).

We read "be thankful," and we nod. That makes sense—for all the reasons we just cited. But "in all circumstances"? *All?* That must be a typo, right? Surely Paul forgot an asterisk and the long list of exceptions and exclusions that apply to such a sweeping statement. How are we supposed to be grateful when we dump a cup of coffee in our lap right before the big presentation? Or be thankful for a thankless, low-paying job? Can we really be thankful when we aren't sure how we're going to make next month's mortgage payment? Or when we learn our ninth grader has been sneaking out at night to meet a group of sketchy friends? Thankful in *"all* circumstances"? Paul? Really?

Thinking I must be missing something, I decided to dig a little deeper. What am I not seeing? What exactly does this phrase mean, and how does this work in real life?

I first examined that bothersome word *all.* Guess what it means in the original Greek? It means "all." No exceptions. Thankfulness *is* to be our around-the-clock mind-set.

Next, I noticed that the command is to "*be* thankful," not to "*feel* thankful." When my youngest son was learning to drive, he pulled our Camry into the carport a little too far—as in all the way into the living room wall. I don't believe God expected me to run out in the front yard and do cartwheels of gladness. I sure didn't *feel* giddy, but I could *be* thankful for lots of reasons: Thankful that no one was hurt; thankful that he didn't continue driving all the way to his bedroom in the rear part of the house; thankful that we had insurance, some money in savings, and kind contractor friends willing to help. The point being, even when we don't *feel* thankful, we can always *be* thankful.

A third thing I noticed is the preposition Paul used: We're called to be thankful "in" all circumstances, not "for" all circumstances. To sing praises *for* an outbreak of evil would be its own kind of evil.

But to find reasons for gratitude *in* the midst of evil is an expression of faith.

And so we come to the great spiritual benefit of a grateful spirit. *Thankfulness makes us and others want to trust God more.* When we grumble incessantly about life's irritations, or when larger trials come, and we succumb to despair and bitterness, aren't we essentially announcing to ourselves and to the watching world, *Do you see my sad life? I'm living proof that a) God isn't good, b) God doesn't know what he's doing, or c) God isn't in control. My pitiful life is what happens when a person decides to trust God.*

Question: What about *that* message would engender faith in anybody, anywhere?

On the other hand, imagine the impact of this kind of response to difficulty: *Okay, Lord, despite how things look—and the way I feel—I'm choosing to believe in this not-so-fun moment that your heart is good and that you are both wise and in control of all things. By faith I say, "Thank you." I'm clinging to your promise that you will somehow work all this together for your glory and my good.* (Romans 8:28.)

This is the sort of thing that's easiest to say when you're *not* in the middle of a crisis, but I'd like to become the sort of person who, if he got cancer, would eagerly tell his neighbors, "I just found out I have cancer. Isn't that interesting? I wonder what God has up his sleeve?"

I want to be a Grateful.

# 21

# WHEN YOU'RE FORCED TO BE AROUND SOMEBODY REALLY ANNOYING

A minister friend told me, "I would absolutely *love* my job…if it weren't for the people." Then he laughed. (Only later did it dawn on me that his laugh didn't mean, "I made a funny joke!" It meant, "I just said a true thing, and what's funny is that you *think* I was joking.")

People. Oh, the humanity! All the Homo sapiens I have to put up with every day. Every day of my existence, I have to deal with Quirky Man, Grand-Canyon-of-Need Person, Mr. Insecure, the 24/7 Critic, and Two-Face.

And that's before anybody else in the house wakes up.

Don't you find that every time you venture out into the world (whether the real world or the World Wide Web), things get "interesting"? You rub shoulders with narcissists. Whiners. Control freaks. Moody coworkers. Drama queens. There's the guy who always says inappropriate things. That boss who won't communicate. That child who won't shut up. Namedropper Woman. Mr.

Has-a-Story-for-Everything. The guy in the next cubicle who talks almost exclusively in movies lines and smells like a survivor from a cologne plant explosion.

Some days, don't you just feel as if you're a cast member in some weird, not-so-funny sitcom?

Here's the thing: Unless you go to a remote island with no neighbors and even fewer dental care providers (ask Tom Hanks how fun *that* was for his character in *Cast Away*), you *have* to be around people. And they're going to drive you nuts—all of them some of the time and some of them all the time.

What to do, then, when you're forced to be around that person who puts the "oy!" in annoying?

Try this life hack, which I call the TLC plan.

## TAKE A QUICK TRIP TO IMAGINATION LAND

When someone annoys me, I imagine the source of my irritation boarding a plane for a five-year stint in Myanmar with the Peace Corps. Not really. (Okay, maybe sometimes.)

No, I imagine that unpleasant person as *a cute toddler*. Seriously. I remind myself that, at one time, the cause of my frown said and did adorable three-year-old things that could make even frustrated patrons at the DMV look up and grin. I know if I could see videos of those precious moments on Facebook, I would sprain my pointer finger hitting the "like" and "share" buttons.

I squinch up my eyes and imagine there's still some of that likability there. Somewhere. Buried *way* up in there. Like gold—deep in the hills, under those mountains, those Himalayas of obnoxiousness. Which leads me to the *L* of the TLC plan. I…

## LOOK FOR THE WONDERFUL WITH THE WEIRD

This is the thing about humans: We are a mixed bag. That singing theologian Paul McCartney was on to something when, in his song "Ebony and Ivory," he crooned about how everyone has both good and bad in them. At least he was right in this sense: We bear the image of God. That's more than good; that's a stunning and glorious truth!

Meanwhile, we are also the sin-damaged offspring of Adam and Eve. Supposedly, Charles Dickens combed his hair obsessively, hundreds and hundreds of times a day. (Ladies, how would you like to be married to *that?*) Yet he somehow found time to also write all those classic books that most high school students *love* (okay, love *to hate*...bad example...scratch that).

Let's take the great inventor Nikola Tesla. He is said to have been a pigeon-loving, workaholic insomniac. (Imagine having that guy as your college roommate! Now imagine having to imagine that *in the dark*—because without Tesla we might not have electricity!)

I promise you, whoever is making you crazy has some upside. You just have to look harder to find it.

## CONSIDER THE HUMBLING TRUTH THAT YOU'RE SOMEONE ELSE'S ANNOYING PERSON

This is maybe the most important aspect of this life hack.

It's normal to think *I am normal; everyone else is weird.*

It's also vain. And false.

I hate to break it to you, but you are *not* normal, and you *do* rub some people the wrong way. If Tesla could have perfected his Thought Bubble Interpretation Device, we'd all be mortified at how much certain people *don't* enjoy having us around.

The great evangelist D.L. Moody seemed to have a good handle on this truth. Rather than fixate on others' shortcomings, he humbly admitted, "I have had more trouble with myself than with any other man I have ever met."

Here's what I'm learning: When I focus on keeping my own unlovely tendencies in check, I'm less bothered by (and less aware of) the flaws of others.

I think the apostle Paul put it best when he wrote, "Make allowance for each other's faults" (Colossians 3:13 NLT). In other words, bear with that annoying person (without turning into a bear yourself). Put up with him or her.

Show a little TLC.

## 22

# WHEN YOUR SOUL IS ALL STIRRED UP

People of faith make pilgrimages to places they consider sacred. Jews and Christians flock to Jerusalem. Muslims go to Mecca. Buddhists visit the Bodhi Tree.[1]

I go to Alluvial Fan in Rocky Mountain National Park (RMNP).

"The Fan," as my family affectionately calls it, came into existence in the summer of 1982 when Lawn Lake Dam, high in the park, suddenly gave way. This geological failure unleashed a wall of water that swept trees and massive boulders four miles down a narrow mountain gorge, all the way to Horseshoe Park in the valley below.

Before it was over, the disaster took the lives of three campers and flooded the town of Estes Park, some five miles east. But out of all that death and destruction came a strange beauty. A picturesque waterfall—Horseshoe Falls—now flows into and through a fan-shaped rock field more than 40 acres in size.

Most tourists will tell you Alluvial Fan is pretty. I'm telling you it's also *holy*, a place where heaven and earth meet.[2] Out of an awful event, a place of awe. I visit every chance I get. I go there to read and ponder; to listen for God's still, small voice; to stack stones like prayers. No telling how many hours I've spent there watching all that clear, cold mountain water dance over the rocks, feeling all those hot tears splash down my cheeks.

Maybe when I go the way of all the earth, my family will scatter my ashes there.

On one of my first visits to RMNP—it was early afternoon—a thunderstorm came out of the west. It rumbled and rolled over the mountains, turning the sky to gray slate. The wind picked up, causing the aspen trees all around us to quake and tremble. Soon the heavens opened.[3]

It rained hard for about an hour. Then this fierce weather system moved east, leaving behind a Colorado bluebird sky. After the storm, the water crashing through the Fan no longer sparkled. It was brown, like coffee with cream. I put my camera away.

The next morning, I was in the park shortly after sunrise. The water cascading through the Fan was still cloudy. But when I returned that evening around sunset, the water was crystal clear again.

It seems to me that storms do three things:
They turn the world dark and ominous.
They lash it fiercely.
They leave it stirred up and mucky.
Metaphorical storms—an angry conflict or unexpected, upsetting news, for example—do the same things to our souls.

Life is good. You're minding your own business when suddenly the sky turns threatening. A storm is coming. You can't stop its advance; you can only hunker down and ride it out. After it's passed, you realize that all the darkness outside has moved inside. Now your heart is a muddy mountain stream, a stirred-up mess, truth and faith bobbing in the murky, churning waters of doubt and fear.

What can calm your soul and clear it up?

On my desk I have a Ball mason jar full of clear creek water and brown sand. I call it my poor (Southern) man's snow globe. When I give it a few violent shakes, all that water and sediment swirl together, the color of chocolate milk.

Then when I set down the jar and go about my business, I behold the power of stillness. In a day or two all that dirt settles. The water once again looks clear enough to drink. (Not that I'm tempted to drink water from a ditch, but you get my meaning.)

This is the hack we need when we're all stirred up inside. (No, not grabbing a jar and heading for the nearest stream—as if a stressed-out soul needs a field trip and a DIY craft.) We need to pull away from all the hubbub, find a peaceful place, and be still.

This is precisely what we read in Psalm 46. This psalm doesn't explicitly mention storms or muddy streams, but it does reference all sorts of world-shaking disasters—earthquakes, crumbling mountains, surging waters...even war. With such calamity as a backdrop, the psalmist then quotes the Lord God Almighty telling his agitated people, "Be still [*relax, let go*], and know that I am God" (verse 10). Jesus said almost the same words—"Hush, be still"—to a fierce storm that was agitating the Sea of Galilee and the hearts of his frantic followers (Mark 4:39 NASB).

At times, I've found it's possible to calm my stirred-up heart in short order. I slip out the door for a walk full of deep breaths, thoughts centered on the Storm Stiller. After three or four trips around the block, the dark fears and cloudy doubts have mostly dropped out of view.

Of course, if you've just come through a more severe storm, the settling process can take longer: a weekend, perhaps even a week. And if you're coming to terms with a major crisis event, you'll need much more time to reach a place of clarity. In that case, I recommend a longer retreat, perhaps even a pilgrimage of sorts. (I can recommend a fantastic place at Rocky Mountain National Park.)

But whether you go or stay put, if your soul is stirred up, it needs to settle. So...

Be still. Relax. Breathe. In time you'll get the clarity you need. You'll be able to see again—and know—that God is still on his throne.

# 23

# WHEN YOU GET AN ENCOURAGING NOTE

You walk out to your mailbox, and there amid all the grocery store circulars, credit card applications, and utility bills is a card-sized, hand-addressed envelope. (Question 1: Who in the world still sends personal notes? Question 2: Why don't we all do this... all the time?)

You're puzzled. It's not your birthday. You don't recognize the handwriting. You tear open the envelope expecting a thank-you note for some recent wedding present or birthday gift. Only that's not what this is.

It's a few lines from a young woman who used to live two doors down. She's starting her pediatric residency next month, and out of the blue she's written you a note about a life-altering interaction in your kitchen more than a decade ago.

She mentions a passing conversation over homemade chocolate chip cookies:

> I was beginning high school and expressing concerns about classes and grades, and I remember you spinning around

from the stove, spatula in hand. You had a stunned look, and you responded in a shocked voice, "You? Worried? Why, you're the smartest and sweetest kid I know—don't tell my kids I said that!" Then, matter-of-factly, you added, "You'll end up in med school one day."

You will never know what you did for my heart in that moment. My home life was chaotic (to say the least), so knowing you believed in me gave me a confidence I'd never had before. Here's the truth: I wouldn't be where I am if not for you. I am forever grateful.

Isn't it strange that while you can't even remember this moment, she has never forgotten it? When a ninth-grade neighbor was floundering, you spoke a couple of sentences of life. Without even realizing it, you nonchalantly threw her a verbal lifeline—and a lantern and a compass all at once! How could you have known she'd cling to your words all these years?

Here's a life hack recommendation: Don't throw such precious notes away. They're holy. Put them in a shoe box. Keep the box somewhere safe. Then add to it. That card you'll get in a few weeks from the grateful parent of the kid you've been teaching—stick that in your box. Put it in there with that sweet letter of appreciation from the small group you led. Slowly fill your box with every uplifting email or affirming card that comes your way.

Why? Because in a decade or so (or maybe in just a few months), you'll find yourself dangling, wondering if your life has mattered. You'll question if you've made a difference. You'll doubt that God could or would use someone like you. In a discouraging world, the words and stories in a box full of memories are like weapons-grade encouragement.

*Encourage* is one of the best words we have, one of the best things we could ever do. It comes from an Old French verb meaning "to put heart or courage into someone." In the New Testament, the Greek word translated *encouragement* conveys the idea of consolation, solace, comfort, and even exhortation. (Sounds a lot like someone serving up warm chocolate chip cookies with a smile and an inspiring challenge, doesn't it?)

One man in the Bible was so good at coming alongside others and putting heart into them that everybody started calling him Barnabas, a nickname that literally means "son of encouragement" (Acts 4:36). In other words, if encouragement had a baby, it would have been this guy.

That's the perfect name for your collection of notes. Call it your "Barnabas File."

But the hack here isn't merely to create such a box. The idea is to make the box and then peruse its contents from time to time. Let it encourage you with the truth that you *have it within you* to mark others in good ways.

Then—and this is big—let what you find in the box challenge you to "excel still more" (1 Thessalonians 4:1 NASB). Make it your daily habit to engage in the beautiful practice of encouragement. Try to give at least one person a "mailbox moment" every day. Start now. Before your head hits the pillow tonight, write a note (or at least send an email or a text) that someone could add to his or her own Barnabas File.

When we encourage others, we end up feeling encouraged ourselves. That's not the main reason we do it, of course. But as perks go, it's a good one.

# 24

# WHEN YOU'RE DISGUSTED WITH YOURSELF BECAUSE OF ALL THE THINGS YOU "SHOULD" BE DOING BUT AREN'T

Carl is a conscientious, well-meaning man. He pays his taxes scrupulously. He flosses religiously. He never kicks his dog. He's a good man with a good heart.

But Carl has a problem. Every day he ends up overwhelmed by all the things he feels he *should* be doing.

Yesterday, for example, he woke up, saw his reflection in the hall mirror, grimaced, and thought, *I should start doing CrossFit... crunches...something!*

In the kitchen, he poured his coffee, unconsciously rubbed his pudgy gut, and mused, *I should stop using half-and-half.*

Carl guiltily carried his mug of creamy coffee to the table. He checked his email, and soon he was lost in a thousand thoughts: *I should respond to this right now, before I forget... I should call him later today... I should read that book... I should check out this conference... I should go to that church event... I should unsubscribe to this newsletter...*

Thirty minutes later he lamented, *I should figure out some way to keep email from dominating my life!*

A few seconds later, an inaudible voice said, *You should check Facebook.*

While scrolling hurriedly through his feed, Carl mumbled things like, "I should take my family there one day... I should 'friend' that guy... I should 'like' that... I should try that diet... I should watch that series on Netflix... I should change my profile picture... Whoa! I should get to work!"

At his job, he could still hear the voices, some from without—*You should check with compliance on that... You should read this report before tomorrow's meeting*—and some from within—*I should have chosen a different career... I should learn some new skills...* (Then, after a tense exchange with his boss, *Maybe I should dust off my résumé.*)

A coworker stuck his head in Carl's doorway and said, "We're eating an early lunch at the Three Caballeros. You should come." A friend texted him and said, "Allyson and I are going to the lake this weekend. You and Fran should join us." Just then Fran texted and said, "Your dad's birthday is in three days! You should stop after work and get him a card."

After work, while inching along in rush-hour traffic, Carl had random thoughts like: *I should walk over and meet the new neighbors tonight... I should get a haircut... I should clean this nasty old truck, and then I should sell it and get a more economical vehicle...* Then, spying a Powerball billboard, he blurted, "It's $357 million? I should stop and get a ticket! Or two."

Pulling into his driveway—without a birthday card but with three lottery tickets—the drumbeat of "shoulds" continued, *You should mow the grass before the neighborhood association files a complaint... You should take the kids to the park, but first you should check the mail...*

After supper, while perusing three requests for donations, he nodded. *I should support these causes.* Then, staring at his checkbook balance, he shook his head. *I should figure out a way to make a little extra money.*

After the kids were asleep, Carl remembered his "work homework" and groaned. After a few seconds, he thought, *Nah, I should set my alarm an hour early and read the report first thing in the morning.*

At the end of a full day, the good man with the good heart fell into bed. It was late. His wife was already sawing logs. Carl felt extremely weary...but even more guilty.

*I didn't floss*, he realized. *I should get up and floss!*

Utterly frustrated, he whispered, "God, my life isn't working. What should I do?"

To his great shock, it was as if God whispered back.

"Stop listening to all those voices telling you all the things you *should* be doing."

Maybe, like Carl, you find yourself fighting chronic, low-grade guilt, with the result that you are constantly kicking yourself for all the ways you feel like you don't measure up. If so, it's time to hack the language of obligation out of your vocabulary. The joy-robbing phrase "I should..." and its cousins "I'm supposed to..." and "I ought to..." need to be 86ed from your life! (Understand, I am not saying that you *should* do this, only that *if you're wise...*)

Jesus didn't come to give us more rules! He came to give us new life...to make us new creatures with new hearts and new desires. His good news is rooted in grace, not guilt. He motivates through delight, not duty. Meaning, followers of Jesus don't ever *have* to read the Bible, go to church, pray, or serve others. On the contrary, we *get* to do those things—and whatever else honors God, blesses others, and brings holy joy to our own souls.

It comes down to this…if the voice telling you what to do is pushy and manipulative, if it's guilt inducing and not grace-giving, you can be sure of this: It's not the Lord's voice.

# 25

# WHEN YOU'RE IRRITATED BY ALL THOSE PESKY PEOPLE IN YOUR WAY

My friend Pat sends me voice memos—via text message.

(I'm such a dinosaur. I didn't even know this was technologically possible. Do you think one day it might be possible to *see the faces* of people we're talking to on our smartphones?)

Pat is smart and hilarious, and he has a big heart for people. So, naturally, I smile whenever I see a new audio text from him on my phone.

Often his messages are *quirky*—like the time he did a spot-on impersonation of Jeff Bridges's courtroom speech from *True Grit*. (Until he fessed up, I was utterly convinced it was an audio clip from the movie.)

Other times his messages are *encouraging*—like when he gave me feedback on something I'd written. Ten minutes passed, and then he sent me a second message—this one longer and gushier. (His affirmation made me want to keep writing deep into the night.)

Occasionally, though, his words are *challenging*. Recently a voice mail/text from him went something like this:

Okay, here's an idea. What if we all made it a practice to pray for the people around us? I mean, the people literally in proximity to us?

You're at a stop light, say, and a bearded guy in a black Mustang convertible is in front of you. He's got all these tattoos, and you don't know anything about him—his background or what he's facing—just that he's in your way (maybe keeping you from turning right on red). What if you just started praying for him? That God would show up in his life and help him and meet his needs?

Or you're in the checkout line and it's long. But instead of getting frustrated, you make the choice to look around and notice the people, who, for reasons only God knows, happen to be at the grocery store with you at that exact moment. Suddenly, you're praying silently for that weary-looking mom who's trying to ride herd on two little hellion kids or for the cashier who might have a hard life.

This would do a couple of things. First, it would change our attitudes. Instead of seeing people as obstacles in our way, we'd see them as precious and unique. Second, people would be getting prayed for all over the place. And God knows we can all use that. So there's our opportunity to change the world. Let's run with it.

My friend Pat is right. If enough people of faith embraced this simple life hack, it really could, really would change the world.

I'm taking the challenge. I'm trying to cultivate the habit of mentioning people to God—whoever he puts in my path—as I go about my day. Not just my family and friends—I already do that—but all the strangers along the way and especially *in* my way.

What if we ran with my friend's idea and started a movement of "guerrilla praying"?

Can you imagine?

# WHEN YOU'RE READY TO QUIT

'm not a betting man, but if I were, I'd wager my most precious assets[1] that you have at least one situation in your life where you're thinking, *This is futile. Why do I keep banging my head against this wall?*

What's that "impossible" challenge for you? Losing weight? Earning an advanced degree? Forging friendships in a new place? Learning a new skill? Landing a better job? Staying in a tough marriage? Getting to know God?

Maybe you've tried to repair a broken relationship—and you've been rebuffed again and again and again. (I know that drill.) Or you've prayed faithfully and fervently about a matter close to your heart. Months or even years later, not a shred of evidence indicates that God has done anything to alter the situation.

*This is pointless,* you think. *I quit!*

I understand that feeling, believe me. But before you throw in the proverbial towel, consider this story.

In 2005, a woman in the South Korean village of Sinchon decided to get her driver's license, but because she had a limited educational background, she failed the written exam.

This is hardly newsworthy, except for the fact that Cha Sa-soon, then in her mid-sixties, decided she would retake the test until she passed. She was tired of spending hours a day riding and waiting on buses.

If we let *x* represent another failed driver's test, here's a snapshot of Ms. Cha's efforts to get her license over the next three or so years:

x x x x x x x x x x x x x x x x x x x x x x x x x x x x x x
x x x x x x x x x x x x x x x x x x x x x x x x x x x x x x
x x x x x x x x x x x x x x x x x x x x x x x x x x x x x x
x x x x x x x x x x x x x x x x x x x x x x x x x x x x x x
x x x x x x x x x x x x x x x x x x x x x x x x x x x x x x
x x x x x x x x x x x x x x x x x x x x x x x x x x x x x x
x x x x x x x x x x x x x x x x x x x x x x x x x x x x x x
x x x x x x x x x x x x x x x x x x x x x x x x x x x x x x
x x x x x x x x x x x x x x x x x x x x x x x x x x x x x x
x x x x x x x x x x x x x x x x x x x x x x x x x x x x x x
x x x x x x x x x x x x x x x x x x x x x x x x x x x x x x
x x x x x x x x x x x x x x x x x x x x x x x x x x x x x x
x x x x x x x x x x x x x x x x x x x x x x x x x x x x x x
x x x x x x x x x x x x x x x x x x x x x x x x x x x x x x
x x x x x x x x x x x x x x x x x x x x x x x x x x x x x x
x x x x x x x x x x x x x x x x x x x x x x x x x x x x x x
x x x x x x x x x x x x x x x x x x x x x x x x x x x x x x
x x x x x x x x x x x x x x x x x x x x x x x x x x x x x x
x x x x x x x x x x x x x x x x x x x x x x x x x x x x x x
x x x x x x x x x x x x x x x x x x x x x x x x x x x x x x
x x x x x x x x x x x x x x x x x x x x x x x x x x x x x x
x x x x x x x x x x x x x x x x x x x x x x x x x x x x x x

Despite some seven hundred failures, Ms. Cha remained undeterred (or, in her son's words, "stubborn"). Word spread about the
cheerful widow in the mountain village south of Seoul who was
determined to get a driver's license. Instructors at the nearby Jeon-
buk Driving School offered assistance. News crews started following
her tenacious efforts, which continued at least twice a week:

*Finally*, at the age of 69, after 959 failed tests (each one costing
her $5), Ms. Cha passed test number 960! All of South Korea cele-
brated her extraordinary perseverance, and the nation's leading car-
maker, the Hyundai-Kia Automotive Group, awarded her a new
vehicle valued at almost $17,000! Her driving school instructors
were euphoric. One of them explained, "We didn't have the guts to
tell her to quit because she kept showing up."[2]

*She kept showing up.* When everything within you is saying,
"That's it. I'm done!" here's the unsophisticated, not-so-ingenious
hack you need: *Keep showing up.*

Once, while teaching about prayer, Jesus told his followers to
imagine a scenario where a friend descends on you in the middle of
the night (Luke 11:5-8). Let's say, Jesus proposed, you have no food
to offer a hungry, unexpected houseguest, so you go to the neighbor's

house, bang on the door, and ask if you can borrow three loaves of bread. And suppose, Jesus continued, that from within the house, your irritated neighbor says, "I don't care if you are my friend and neighbor; it's late! My family is already asleep, and the house is locked up tight. So, no, I'm not going to help you. Not tonight. Go away!"

Jesus let that hypothetical situation sink in for a few seconds. Then he concluded his teaching with these words: "I tell you this. Though he won't do it for friendship's sake, *if you keep knocking long enough*, he will get up and give you whatever you need because of your *shameless persistence*" (Luke 11:8 NLT, emphases added).

*Shameless persistence.* If you ask me, that's one of the best phrases ever. It means having the tenacious audacity to continue knocking. It's the cheeky resolve to keep showing up (or looking up or speaking up) regardless of what anyone else might be thinking or saying. It's that old cliché "Try and try again" on steroids.

Shameless persistence is how a tiny-but-tough South Korean widow got her driver's license. It's how Thomas Edison *finally* figured out the light bulb. And it's how you will...do what?

What's the desirable thing that eludes you? The painful endeavor you're ready to abandon because you keep failing?

Whatever it is, Jesus—and Ms. Cha—would say, "Don't give up. Try again. Shamelessly knock some more. Show up one more time."

Walk through those gym doors again today. Park your buns in front of those textbooks one more time. Make another sweet gesture (because even if it doesn't bring down the whole wall, it might loosen one small brick).

You've applied for 117 jobs and have nothing to show for your efforts? Okay. That means a) you are relentless, and b) it's time to open your laptop again, do another internet search, and send out résumé number 118.

Still no answer to prayer? For heaven's sake, don't quit! Jesus himself said to be shameless! Persist. Audaciously ask again.

And if nothing happens? You can try again tomorrow.

# 27

# WHEN YOU'VE DECIDED YOU HAVE NOTHING TO OFFER ANYONE

'm guessing you're like me at least in this one way: At times you catch yourself shaking your head at the talented people around you and thinking, *What do I have to offer? I'm not good at anything!*

My friend Chris, for example, is an outstanding communicator. He's smart. He's funny. He's a gifted storyteller. Unlike me, he never needs notes, he never gets his "tang tungled," and he never says "uh" or "um" when he speaks. Sometimes when he's doing his thing, I'll glance around at the congregation and marvel at how engaged everyone is. People are leaning in and nodding all over the room. Nodding *off*? Never! Trust me, when Chris is teaching, nobody is making a grocery list or checking Instagram.

Another friend of mine, Dee, is a world-class musician and theatrical director. He's married to Tami, a gifted singer and comedic actress. No exaggeration—they could be living in New York City and "breaking their legs" nightly on Broadway. Instead, they bless our community with their skills. I know, I know. Typically, artsy types roll their eyes at community theater productions. Not in our city, they don't. Not when it's a Dee and Tami production.

Without a doubt, you have folks like this in your life. People with astonishing abilities—they can speak five languages, or they can save lives by performing neurosurgery, like my doctor friend Mike. Maybe they excel in a sport—like the three sons of my friends Shawn and Toya who all play in the NBA. Or they launch a new *successful* business about every other month, like my friends Brent and Amy.

When you're surrounded by uber-gifted people, it's easy to feel like a talentless schmuck. If that's an occasional struggle for you, I have a spiritual life hack for you—with two parts.

First, *stop comparing!* Comparing is silly—sort of like the carpenter who starts feeling inferior when the electricians and plumbers show up on a job site. *But they're responsible for lights and flushing toilets!* Yes, Mr. Carpenter, and guess what else is true? Walls and cabinets are important too.

The reality is that God designed and assigned you to do things only you can do. This puts you in a class all by yourself. It means you're incomparable. And that means measuring yourself against other people to determine your worth or draw conclusions about your significance is foolish if not downright sinful. Cut it out!

Second, when you catch yourself thinking you have no contribution to make, *take inventory of your unique life and soul.*

This exercise isn't hard to do, and I always find it encouraging. Grab paper and a pen. Survey your wholly original life and consider the remarkable smorgasbord of gifts, talents, and resources you've been given. The categories that follow aren't an exhaustive list, but they're enough to jog your thinking.

- *Personality.* What's your temperament, your essential makeup? Are you introverted or extroverted? (FYI, some of the world's most influential people are quiet, not gregarious.) Are you people focused or task oriented? Driven or laid-back? A thinker or a feeler? Remember, there's no such thing as a "right" personality.

- *Natural abilities.* God gave you certain built-in capacities. Are you physically coordinated? Naturally funny? Artistic? Verbal? Analytical? Detail oriented? A born problem solver? Every one of these aptitudes (and the ten thousand I didn't name) is important and useful.

- *Spiritual gifts.* If you're a believer in Jesus, the Spirit of God Almighty lives in you, and he has given you at least one supernatural ability for serving the body of Christ (Romans 12; 1 Corinthians 12; Ephesians 4; 1 Peter 4). It might be leading, giving lavishly, sharing the Good News, serving, encouraging, showing mercy, or something else. To say you have *nothing* to contribute is to deny this biblical reality.

- *Acquired skills.* What are some things you've *learned* to do? Work on cars? Sew? Garden? Edit videos? Bake? Do CPR? Build web pages? Just because you can't fill an auditorium with people paying $200 each to watch you make Excel spreadsheets doesn't mean that skill (or any other) is not valuable or not needed.

- *Experiences.* Maybe you were an only child (or like my buddy Barkef, one of *12*!). Perhaps you were a "military brat" and grew up all over the world. Don't discount for a moment any of your unique life experiences. God wants to use all those details in wildly creative ways to accomplish his will—both in your life and in the world.

- *Hardships.* Raised in poverty? Child of an alcoholic parent? Widowed? Cancer survivor? Living with a disability? Those realities hurt. Yet God uses hard things not only to shape us but also to equip us to comfort others who are suffering in similar ways. The lessons you've learned from your difficulties—and even your failures— are invaluable!

- *Blessings.* Maybe you're healthy and well educated. You have a happy family, a home with spare bedrooms or an empty garage apartment, a good income. For heaven's sake—literally—what could you do with such advantages and resources?

We could keep going—your stage of life (young and single? empty nester? retired?), your connections, the issues you care deeply about (that nobody else around you seems to even notice), the unique ways you long to make a difference in the world—but you get the idea.

Take inventory. Instead of noticing what others have and you don't, how about focusing on everything God has dropped in your lap?

It's a whole lot more than you think.

# 28

# WHEN YOU FIND YOURSELF A LITTLE TOO CONCERNED ABOUT "HIM," "HER," OR "THEM"

C an you imagine if social media had been a thing during the time of Christ? From what the Gospels tell us about the 12 disciples, it's not hard to envision a scenario like this:

Jesus, after a night of prayer on some Galilean mountainside, approaches his disciples. None of the 12 even notices the Lord's arrival because each is facedown in his smartphone. Thomas is feeling insecure and embarrassed because nobody—not one single person—commented on his thoughtful Facebook post about faith and doubt. At the same time, he's both mystified and miffed that 137 people liked—and 16 of them shared—a silly video that Bartholomew posted last night about fainting sheep.

John is whispering to James, "How in the world does Peter, of all people, have so many Twitter followers?" James, unfortunately, doesn't even hear his brother because he's deep in thought, wondering what the consequences will be from John the Baptist's tweet storm about Herod's illicit relationship with Herodias.

Meanwhile, Matthew has just finished reading Simon the Zealot's latest emoji-filled, all-caps rant against ROMAN OPPRESSION and is muting (not blocking) him on Twitter and unfollowing (but not unfriending) him on Facebook. Andrew is on Instagram posting a picture of the group's fish-and-bread breakfast—which is almost identical to all the other breakfast pictures he's posted each morning for the last two weeks. Judas Iscariot, peering over his shoulder at the group, sighs, rolls his eyes, and opens Denarium, a new financial app he uses to monitor his latest crypto-currency investments.

Jesus surveys his little band and briefly considers calling down a plague on the internet.

This isn't a screed about the evils of social media. (Although I *do* sometimes think that if the devil had tempted Jesus a fourth time, it would have been to try to convince him to create a Facebook account.)

This is about being other-centered in the best possible way.

Other-centeredness, you see, comes in two forms. One variety makes everybody—God included—smile. This is a Philippians 2:3-4 kind of relating. Your spouse reads on Facebook that a former neighbor is in trouble…and immediately jumps into the car. Or your mom hears about a financial need…and whips out her checkbook. Or you find out friends are finally expecting their first child after lots of fertility issues…and you show up at their house with a cake and balloons.

The second kind of "other-centeredness" is not so lovely. Like the first, it closely monitors what's happening in the lives of others. But it rarely amounts to anything more than a detached nosiness. Worse, it can quickly turn us into critics and second-guessers.

The first variety serves. It sees the needs of others and rolls up its sleeves. The second variety stalks. It sees the activities of others and makes catty comments or quietly seethes.

As I mentioned before, the book of John records an incident involving Peter (and six other disciples) meeting and eating with the resurrected Christ on the shore of the Sea of Galilee. After breakfast, Jesus initiated a conversation with Peter that was both painful and gracious. In short, he let Peter know that, despite his shocking denials about knowing him (Matthew 26:69-75; Mark 14:66-72; Luke 22:54-62; John 18:15-18,25-27), he was still a valued member of the team. He restored Peter, and then he talked about Peter's future, alluding vaguely to his death.

Perhaps Peter was tired of being the center of attention, embarrassed by all those eyeballs staring a hole through him as Jesus hinted at his recent failures (and spoke cryptically about his murky future). He turned his face away. When he did, he saw John. Immediately, he tried to shift the spotlight and change the subject: "Lord, what about him?" (John 21:21).[1]

Jesus's reply was epic: "If I want him to remain alive until I return, what is that to you? As for you, follow me" (verse 22 NLT). In other words, "Peter! John's life, his future, his actions—that's none of your business. All that is between him and me. Quit worrying about what others are up to. Focus on the task I've given you—feeding my flock."

Keeping tabs on those around us is a practice as old as the human race (Genesis 4). It used to be that when the Jones family bought a fancy new car, most of the neighbors either tried to keep up or descended into envy. In the age of social media, this phenomenon is magnified a thousandfold. Not so long ago, if you wanted to see what your neighbors were eating for supper, you had to be creepy and go peek in their dining room window! Or if you wanted to gawk at strangers' vacation photos, you had to land a job at a photo-processing store. Not anymore. Now we can see almost anything about anybody with a few clicks.

It's a slippery slope, isn't it? We join social media, we say, to keep up with old friends. But if we're not careful, our "curiosity and concern" can slowly morph into voyeurism and then criticism. We can become other-centered in the worst way—nosy rubberneckers who are so obsessed with the lives of others that we forget what God has told us to do.

When we find ourselves starting to focus unhealthily on "him" or "her" or "them," two hacks can help.

The first is to remember Jesus's stern words to Peter: "What is that to you?" I'm also challenged by the question Paul asked some self-appointed hall monitors in Rome: "Who are you to judge someone else's servant?" (Romans 14:4). And I'm convicted by my wise wife's comment: "I can't keep my own life straight—why would I try to police someone else's?"

A second way to combat this tendency of fixating on the lives of others—especially if it happens mostly online—is to take periodic breaks from social media. I didn't grow up in a faith tradition that observes Lent, but last year from Ash Wednesday to Easter Sunday, I gave up Twitter, Facebook, and Instagram. For those six weeks, I didn't post anything and didn't check to see what others were posting.

It was heavenly.

Jesus didn't have to talk about the dangers of social media with his first-century followers, but something tells me he wants us modern-day believers to use it to love others well or not use it at all.

# 29

# WHEN YOU DON'T FEEL LIKE DOING WHAT YOU NEED TO DO

Confession is good for the soul—even if it's not always so great for the reputation. So be it. I'll take my chances. Here's my confession: I don't always *feel* like doing what would bring the most honor to God and the most blessing to others.

Don't mishear me. Some days I wake up enthusiastic about reading the Bible and eager to talk with God, or happy to help people in need, or give money to a good cause.

But I can't lie. Other times, I don't—to quote an old football coach—"have a want" to do what's right and best. Far too often, I don't *feel* like biting my tongue. Or I'm not exactly *eager* to trust God in a risky situation. Sometimes I scan my soul for some warm spiritual feeling to tap into, only to find there's no deep passion there.

I would ask if you ever have that experience—except I already know the answer to that question.

Can we just be honest about feelings? Our emotions are like a roomful of busy toddlers. Wiggling and wriggling all over creation, our feelings constantly climb and fall, come and go, coo and cry. While one is making a scene—and your back is turned addressing that situation—another one quietly goes missing. The good news: Our emotions *do* take short catnaps. The bad news: They never settle down all at once. Right when you manage to calm down one, two others unexpectedly kick up a ruckus. Our toddler-like feelings can both delight us and drive us nuts, often simultaneously! Our best hope? What a weary, veteran nursery worker once said: "I can't control them completely, but I can at least avoid letting them take over."

Precisely.

Here's how the Bible presents God-honoring spirituality: the people of God living *with* great emotion but not living *by* their emotion. In other words, feelings are always acknowledged, but they're never allowed to dictate behavior. Why not? Because feelings are notoriously fickle and unpredictable. Today you may be overflowing with a deep, heartfelt love for God. Tomorrow your heart might be like a frozen river.

Okay, then. If feelings aren't supposed to dictate our actions, what is? One of the most famous and oft-quoted verses in the Bible puts it this way: "The righteous will live by his faith" (Habakkuk 2:4 NASB).[1] The apostle Paul echoed this idea, writing, "We live by faith, not by sight" (2 Corinthians 5:7). No matter how powerful our feelings, our faith must always call the shots. With this mind-set, the psalmist David honestly confessed, "I am in distress; my eyes grow weak with sorrow…My life is consumed by anguish" before rendering his decision: "But I trust in you, LORD" (Psalm 31:9-10,14). And, of course, the ultimate example is Jesus in Gethsemane essentially telling the Father, "I'm not overflowing with eagerness here. I don't exactly *want* to go through what you're asking me to go through," but then "Yet not my will, but yours be done" (Luke 22:42).

Do you see? Two things are true about our fluctuating feelings: We don't have to deny them, and we also don't have to let them boss us around. Because we know that faith alone pleases God (Hebrews 11:6), we let faith have the final word. When we're animated by strong spiritual passions, wonderful! And when we feel dead inside, that's okay too. We live by faith, not feelings. As C.S. Lewis noted, "Feelings come and go, and when they come a good use can be made of them: they cannot be our regular spiritual diet."[2]

What's the hack when you're not exactly oozing with holy desire?

My wife and I still chuckle about an incident from early in our marriage. Neither of us remembers the details, only that we were far enough into "holy matrimony" that flirty winks had finally given way to frustrated eye rolls. Reality had taken romance out into the back alley and was roughing it up pretty good. As I recall, at the end of a brief spat, Cindi looked at me and said, rather unconvincingly, "I love you." And I responded flatly, "I love you too…*by faith.*"

We burst out laughing. In hindsight, it was a great epiphany for two newlyweds. How easy it is to love when you're churning with hormones. What about when you don't feel anything? Or worse, when you feel irritated and tired?

What we each were communicating was something like this:

In this moment, I honestly don't feel a lot of warm, ooey-gooey feelings for you in my heart. But that's okay. I made a commitment to you in front of God and a bunch of witnesses, so I'm not going anywhere. With God's help, I will be faithful to you. I will keep my promises. I don't need heartthrobs and candlelight to do what's right. In this moment, I will live—and love—by *faith*.

As phrases go, *by faith* isn't especially long or catchy. But what a hack it is! What power it contains. What a difference it makes when we make it part of our daily vernacular—and say it from the heart:

- I honestly *feel* like sinning here—saying something petty and mean, or turning the conversation in a self-centered direction, or misusing one of God's good gifts [food or sex or my children] to make myself feel better. But *by faith* I'm going to say no to that temptation and yes to Christ.

- I don't *feel* like going to work today, but *by faith* I will show up, trusting God to give me strength and joy and believing that he can and will work through me to bless others.

- I don't *feel* like reading to the kids tonight—I'm pooped. But *by faith* I will spend a few sweet minutes snuggled up to them with their favorite books—and who knows how God might use that time in their little hearts?

- I don't *feel* like addressing yesterday's big blow-up with my sister. But *by faith*, I'm going to grab my phone right now and give her a call, trusting God to give me

humility, wisdom, and a calm spirit—and to help me
say what I need to say.

Maybe today you *feel* like doing something wrong. Or maybe
you *don't feel* like doing the one thing you most need to do. Or perhaps all you feel is scared or tired or blah.

It's okay to admit such feelings. But when all our talk of feelings
is finished, we're called to live by faith. And ironically, as we live by
faith, we often find holy passions returning to our hearts.

# WHEN YOU'RE IN A PSALM 98 WORSHIP SERVICE WITH A PSALM 88 HEART

s it just my imagination, or have we seen an increase in Psalm 98 worship services over the last few years?

If you've never heard that phrase—*Psalm 98 worship services,* and I'm guessing you haven't since I just made it up—you need to know that Psalm 98 calls for singing "to the LORD a new song" (verse 1).[1] It emphasizes the "marvelous things" God has done, such as providing salvation, being faithful to his people, and ruling the world justly. Toward the end of the psalm, the Spirit-guided writer gets over-the-top exuberant, calling on *all creation* to join in glad celebration.

I'm convinced that worship pastors read this psalm and reason, *If the mountains are commanded to sing, and the rivers are expected to clap their hands, then, by golly, I'm not about to let our people sit there with their arms folded!* And so, in a Psalm 98 service, everyone is urged to stand and get excited, raise their hands, and "shout for joy."

These kinds of services are exactly what the psalm describes: "jubilant!" They're typically lively, upbeat, and loud. A church I visited recently gave out earplugs at the door. I am not kidding. Instead of candles and incense, we got concert lighting and smoke machines. It was sort of like a pep rally for God.

To be sure, plenty of times I've attended Psalm 98 services out of anticipation (*I can't* wait *to do this*). Other Sundays I've gone largely out of obligation (*I probably* need *to do this*).

Lately, it's been the latter. More battle than joy. More duty than desire. As many Sundays as not, I drive to church not because I want to learn another new song or because I feel like shouting and clapping but because Christians are called to gather together (Hebrews 10:24-25). I go *by faith.* And I go because I'm scared of what my heart might become if I stopped going.

Some Sundays I think, *Maybe if I drag my raggedy soul up the street, God will touch it, heal it, fill it, and transform it. Maybe today I'll hear his voice in an unmistakable way. Through the preaching, maybe—a word of comfort or rebuke, it doesn't matter. I can always use plenty of both. Probably the music will be loud—and new to me—but maybe a song lyric will remind me of a spiritual truth I need. Perhaps entering and leaving, I'll have an encouraging foyer conversation with a fellow struggler.*

My guess is that you sometimes find yourself in an upbeat, Psalm 98 worship setting and feel:

- *Like an actor*—because that smile you forced as you walked in the door is not at all indicative of what's truly going on in your heart.

- *Like a fraud*—because even though the worship is on

fire, your soul isn't. (Those lyrics about God's great
love—though objectively true—ring hollow. And honestly, how could you possibly—with a straight face
today of all days—sing about having deep trust in God?)

- *Like an outsider or a defect*—because as you stand there
uncomfortably among all the raised arms and blissful
expressions, it's obvious you're not "in the club." It feels
like that time you gamely tried to celebrate with two
friends who just found out they were pregnant as you
were quietly mourning your own inability to conceive.

In times like that—when I find myself feeling like an Eeyore in a
roomful of worshipping Tiggers[2]—Psalm 88 is my go-to heart hack.

A quick note about Psalms: According to BibleGateway (bible
gateway.com), no book of Scripture is more read. Why is it so
beloved? Because these 150 ancient Jewish prayer-poems cover the
full range of human experience. They put words to feelings we all
experience at various times.

It's been suggested that we could divide the psalms into two
broad categories: those that essentially say "Hallelujah!" (either
praising the character of God or expressing thanks for his blessings)
and those that basically say "Help!" (asking for God's intervention).
That's an oversimplification—clearly, other types of psalms exist (for
example, wisdom psalms and messianic psalms, and royal psalms)—
but all in all, that's a fairly accurate classification.

Psalm 88 is one of the "Help!" songs—what scholars call a
*lament* psalm. The lament psalms were written in the face of dire
situations, some personal and the others national. The gist? "God,
I/we are in a terrible mess. Won't you rescue me/us?"

Now, here's a startling truth that most Christians either don't know or don't seem to remember: Roughly one-third of Israel's national hymnbook is made up of lament psalms! They're not glib and giddy compositions. They're not triumphant expressions of faith. They're often grim and desperate.

And the grimmest and most desperate of them all? That would be Psalm 88. The author of that composition speaks of a soul that is "overwhelmed with troubles." He likens himself to a dead man in a deep pit. The reward for all his faithful praying? Silence. He bluntly questions the God he can't find, the God who seems deaf to his cries. Can you imagine your church kicking off its worship service this coming Sunday with a song that features a line that says, "Why, LORD, do you reject me and hide your face from me?" (verse 14). How about one that ends with these lyrics: "Darkness is my closest friend" (verse 18)?

Would that feel like worship to you? Yet, according to the Bible, those lyrics are from one of the top 150 worship songs of all time.

I love Psalm 88 because of how it hacks my understanding of worship. Worship doesn't always have to be a raucous Psalm 98 clap-fest—nor should it be. The message of the lament psalms is this: Come as you are. And when you arrive, don't hide a heart that's broken behind a big, inauthentic grin. Don't be a fake. Worship is more than raising your hands while you sport an expression of ecstasy. Sometimes worship is asking God, *Where are you?* while you sob uncontrollably.

It's okay to bring your troubled, grieving soul into worship.

Come to think of it, where else could you or should you bring it?

# 31

# WHEN PRODUCTIVITY STARTS TO BECOME A PROBLEM

A few years ago I came across a guy online who is a "productivity guru." You know the type: high achiever—probably a "3" on the Enneagram—always "working smarter, not harder" and "getting more done in less time." These kinds of efficiency experts are so efficient that they're able to blog daily and release a new podcast weekly, and still have time to whip out bestselling books, lead live webinars, speak at national conferences, and pose for perfect website pictures with their smiling families.

This guy got my attention. He has an impressive résumé, and swarms of successful people swear by him. Plus, he talked about "revenue streams."

God knows—slug that I sometimes am—I can always stand to be more organized and productive and motivated (and have more revenue streaming in). I promptly signed up to get his emails.

Here is what I quickly discovered: This guy is bona fide. He's knowledgeable and highly creative. He sent me loads of quality content, much of it free. But honestly? After a while, it was overwhelming. He was sending me something new almost every day: a new blog post with a "game-changing" idea to think about. Three new executive skills I should learn. Five new productivity tools to add to my repertoire. A brand-new online course I should hurry and sign up for while the price is only $199.

I tried to keep up—I promise I did. But after a couple of months, I was exhausted—and more paralyzed than productive. I didn't have time to process and put into practice the deluge of efficiency hacks this guru was sending me daily and still live my life. With each new tip or course offering, I found myself groaning. Turns out I was *not* productive at learning how to be productive.

I unsubscribed.

This is *not* a soapbox rant against hustling or accomplishing goals. Planning, within limits, is a good thing. We have this one brief life, and we should make the most of it.

But sometimes we become fanatical in the quest for productivity and efficiency. When we do, we stop seeing time for the wondrous gift it is. Rather than an elegant, ontological environment for pondering and exploring—and enjoying—the great mysteries of life, time becomes a bitter adversary we must conquer. *Leisure* becomes a dirty word. The clock is reduced to a cruel taskmaster, each tick another command to "Hurry up!" Thus, we face the never-ending search for time-saving tactics and strategies to streamline our lives and pack in more.

I'm guessing it's possible to hack your life until it's composed of nothing but shortcuts. But race breathlessly through enough shortcuts, and you'll end up as exhausted as you would have been if you'd remained inefficient! Lily Tomlin once said, "The trouble with the rat race is that even if you win, you're still a rat."

Maybe productivity gurus should be required—like the big pharmaceutical companies—to disclose the downside of all their prescriptions for "doing more in less time":

> Possible side effects of *Productivium* include disappointment—because not all users can expect the same results. Many experience relational stress, inability to feel wonder, and elevated frustration levels when their productivity is thwarted by unforeseen events.
>
> *Achievementia* has been shown to result in headaches, nervous stomach, gross insensitivity to others [blah, blah, blah].

I'm no longer convinced that productivity and quick efficiency are inherently virtuous. Here's why: In the effort to "do a lot and do it fast," I've seen well-meaning people (including the guy whose face I shave most mornings) morph into wild-eyed, goal-oriented tyrants. Productivity can become a kind of addiction, wreaking havoc on your soul. And an obsession with efficiency can metastasize into the ugliest kind of impatience. Gandhi was right when he said, "There is more to life than increasing its speed."

It comes down to this: Do we want to approach our days with a whip and a chair, trying to back them into a corner to show them who's boss? Do we want to put our one and only life in a headlock? Or do we want to enjoy life?

If striving to be more productive has left you frustrated and discouraged, or weary and empty, here's the spiritual hack you need: Give yourself permission to be nonproductive for at least half an hour.

I'm serious. Stop what you're doing. Just *stop*. Stop being so doggone responsible. Declare yourself temporarily off duty.[1] For 30 whole minutes, forget all your time-saving strategies, daily objectives, and weekly goals. Take that precious to-do list—and stick it... um, you know, in your bottom drawer.

Walk outside. Sit in the grass. Close your eyes. Breathe deeply. Listen. Feel the wind or the sun's rays or, if you're lucky, the raindrops or snowflakes on your skin. Open your eyes. Notice your surroundings.

Look down. Find a bug doing the sorts of things bugs do. Watch it for a minute. Imagine for two more minutes what bugs do for fun.

Look around. Observe how the leaves on a nearby tree sway in the breeze. Pay attention to one leaf. Don't worry about having to rake it or blow it off your lawn in coming months. Just sit there with it.

Look up. Enjoy the blue sky, the clouds, and the birds. Consider that the earth on which you sit is hurtling nonstop through space at 67,000 mph. That's fast enough. You don't have to race around on top of that.

Pray. Thank God for the overlooked gift of being able to stop doing and just be. Thank him for the fact that when you did that for 30 measly minutes, the world didn't implode. Thank him for the truth that your worth and his love are not contingent on how effective you are or how much you get done.

I'll end with an anecdote, an encouragement, and a theory.

*The anecdote:* A year or so after I unsubscribed from the productivity guru's emails, he wrote again. This time he was offering a new course about how to avoid doing so much that you burn out. I could only shake my head and smile at the irony.

*The encouragement:* If you *do* happen to find some time

management app or eBook or productivity hack that enhances your life, God bless you! By all means, use it with gratitude. All I'm saying here—as crazy as it sounds—is that sometimes less really is more. And sometimes inefficiency is a blessing, not a curse.

*The theory:* I have a strong sense that when we get to heaven, we're going to learn that God paints those outrageous sunsets in the western sky because he wants people to cease all their time saving and box checking and do nothing for 30 whole minutes but sit back in slack-jawed awe.

# 32

# WHEN YOU'RE
# STARTING SOMETHING

Think of all the things people *start* on any given day. While you're starting your regular morning workout, your neighbor is starting her car (so she can get to the office and start work a little early). Friends across the country are starting their vacation. A coworker is starting a diet.

In roughly an hour, just a block over, a ten-month-old rug rat will start walking. Midmorning at a medical facility across town, a nervous, middle-aged mom will start her first round of chemo. At lunch, two sharp young self-starter types will agree to start a start-up.

After work, your neighbor will rush home to start dinner, and her two kids, instead of starting on their homework, will start arguing. A mile away, in a hip coffee shop, two strangers will start a conversation (and in a couple of weeks, start dating). Later, in an apartment uptown, a frisky young married couple will start a new human being!

We are a race of *starters*. We are forever starting things: assignments and fires, new hobbies and new habits. Sometimes a regular

Joe starts a ball rolling, never imagining that what he just started will grow into a giant movement!

You can't not be a starter. Waking up in the morning equals starting a new day. During that new day, you'll start conversations, maybe a new friendship. You'll start working on something—perhaps starting from scratch, often starting at the place you left off the day before.

Whatever it is you're starting—your day, a new job or new year, a meeting, a negotiation, a healthy habit, a class, or an interview—you want to get off to a flying start. (The last thing in the world you want is to start *tongues wagging*.[1])

Can a spiritual hack help you do that?

You bet.

Around AD 57, the apostle Paul started something—his "magnum opus," known as the epistle to the Romans. His goal through this lengthy letter was to help the Christians in Rome better understand what people sometimes call "the Good News": why Jesus came to earth, died, and rose from the dead.

Eugene Peterson has paraphrased Paul's explanation of the Christian faith this way:

> Since we've...proved that we are utterly incapable of living the glorious lives God wills for us, God did it for us. Out of sheer generosity he put us in right standing with himself. A pure gift. He got us out of the mess we're in and restored

us to where he always wanted us to be. And he did it by means of Jesus Christ. God sacrificed Jesus on the altar of the world to clear that world of sin. Having faith in him sets us in the clear (Romans 3:23-25 MSG).

How remarkable! Paul was saying in so many words that when we trust in Jesus, we get a fresh start with God. And we start over with more than just a clean slate; we also receive a brand-new life! This means we don't have to keep living the way we used to live. In Christ, we have new power to start living in new ways. Given these realities, Paul goes on to tell those ancient believers (and us):

> Do not go on presenting the members of your body to sin as instruments of unrighteousness; but present yourselves to God as those alive from the dead, and your members as instruments of righteousness to God (Romans 6:13 NASB).

Present yourself and "the members of your body...as instruments of righteousness." *This* is the powerful reminder we need at the start of a day, a tense meeting, a date, or a project. This is the hack that can make a difference for starters everywhere. For me, it takes the form of a simple, head-to-toe prayer that goes something like this:

> *Dear God, here at the start of _____, I want to give myself to you one more time. Thank you for taking away my old life and giving me new life in Christ. Thank you that I don't have to live for myself and give in to sinful impulses. Thank you for the wild promise that you can use me for your eternal purposes.*
>
> *Right now, will you take every part of me? Fill my mind with your thoughts and my heart with your love. Lord, I present my eyes to you. May they see everything—you, the world, people,*

*situations, me—as you see. Take my ears. Let me hear your voice above all the loud and conflicting voices in the world. Make me an attentive listener to others also, so that I can be sensitive to their needs.*

*Here's my mouth, God. Please, take control of it. Set a guard over it. If I speak, let me speak words prompted only by your Spirit. Take my hands as well. Animate them. Whether I hug or lift or carry or type, let me do so in a way that honors you and blesses others.*

*Last, I give you my feet. Grant me the humility and courage to go where you want me to go and to serve as you wish me to serve.*

Start using this hack in the next couple of days before you start doing whatever it is you need to start doing. Then watch what happens.

## 33

# WHEN THINGS IN YOUR LIFE ARE SHAKY

n college, I took two whole geology classes. That's not enough training to land a job as a volcanologist, but those classes provided more than enough lectures for me to learn this *scientific* fact: The three kinds of rock are *pebbles*, *stones*, and *boulders*.[1]

Since college, I've discovered a helpful hack to go along with my vast geological expertise:

*Always keep a rock nearby.*

What's not to love about rocks? Skipping a flat stone across a pond. Hearing that cool clacking-clunking sound when you stack big rocks one on top of the other. Watching gravel bounce gracefully out of the dump truck in front of you and...terrible example, never mind.

It's true that pebbles can chip your windshield, stones can break your bones, and falling boulders on mountain highways can squash your SUV. Nevertheless, I maintain that rocks have way more upside than downside.

- *Rocks offer protection.* Why do bighorn sheep and mountain goats make their homes in rocky terrain? Probably for the same reason manufacturers of spare key hiders make them to look like rocks.

- *Rocks are synonymous with stability.* What's the first thing engineers, architects, and builders do at the start of a new construction project? They either a) anchor their new structure to the "bedrock" deep within the earth's surface or b) pour a concrete foundation, which is nothing more than a big, flat, man-made rock. When we want to commend a person (or a pickup truck) for being steady and dependable, we say what? That he, she, or it is "like a rock."

- *Rocks are enduring.* Do you know how old Stonehenge is? Believe it or not, those massive sarsen stones standing in a mysterious circle just west of Amesbury, England, have been watching empires rise and fall for some five thousand years and counting! Weighing 25 to 40 tons each, those slabs aren't going anywhere anytime soon.

- *Rocks are pretty and valuable.* How do we respond when beaming brides-to-be thrust their dazzling, two-carat engagement rings in our faces? "Whoa!" we exclaim. "What a *rock!*"

- *Rocks have a wide variety of uses.* What do you need? A reliable paperweight? A durable and beautiful kitchen counter? Rocks are your ticket. Need building material for a lasting memorial? (Hint: You don't want plastic or plywood or pressboard for that. You want rock.)

- *Rocks are spiritual.* No kidding, the Bible is *full* of rocks. In Genesis, for example, God appears to Jacob one night in a dream. The next morning Jacob wakes up and takes the stone he's just used as a makeshift pillow and turns it into a memorial pillar (Genesis 28). Centuries later, in the wilderness, God gives Moses the supernatural ability to make water flow from a rock (Exodus 17:6). A short time after that, at Sinai, he gives Moses his law on "two tablets…of stone, written with the finger of God" (Exodus 31:18 ESV).

  After crossing the Jordan River, Joshua has the people erect a big pile of stones to commemorate their arrival in the promised land (Joshua 4). Later, with a single, smooth stone, the slingshot-wielding David dispatches the giant Goliath (1 Samuel 17:40-50). In the Psalms—and this is most important—David refers again and again to God as his Rock (Psalm 18:2,31,46; 19:14; 28:1; 31:2-3; 62:1-2,6-7; 144:1). The Old Testament also speaks of a coming cornerstone (Psalm 118:22; Isaiah 8:14; 28:16), which the New Testament apostles identify as Jesus Christ (Matthew 21:42; Romans 9:33; 1 Peter 2:6). Even believers in Jesus are referred to as living stones, and God is said to be building us together into a spiritual house (1 Peter 2:4-10).

These are just a few of the reasons I keep rocks handy—and why you should too. Place them on your desk or dining table, even in your vehicle's console. In a world where so much is temporary and trivial, where circumstances shift and situations feel fragile, seeing—better yet, clutching—a solid, heavy old rock is one hack of a powerful reminder.

Nobody likes a rock in his or her shoe. But a rock in your pocket? That's a different story. When your family is quaking or your finances are unstable, or when a friend's health situation is deteriorating and your faith is shaky, you can take your rock in hand and pray things like:

- *God, help me remember today that you are my Rock, my hiding place, my refuge.*

- *Father, give me a faith that's solid and substantive like this rock. Give me faith that could move a whole mountain of rock like this.*

- *Jesus, give me the wisdom and the will to cling to you today in the same way I'm holding on to this rock.*

- *O gracious Lord, my world seems like it's crumbling. Set my feet on a rock and make my footsteps firm. Lead me to the Rock that is higher than I.*

- *God, if I speak today, may my words carry weight and give comfort and strength.*

Keeping a rock close by isn't a gimmick. Picking it up is not the Christian version of rubbing one of those worry stones they sell in tourist gift shops out West. It's simply a way of remembering that God is like a rock—only infinitely more so. He's strong. Weighty. Enduring. Dependable. And he can make us like that too.

## 34

# WHEN EVERYTHING SEEMS DOOMY AND GLOOMY

At his first inauguration in 1933, U.S. President Franklin D. Roosevelt famously said, "The only thing we have to fear is fear itself." Not quite a century later, the internet tells us the only thing we have to fear is pretty much everything.

"Our overcrowded, burning, quaking, flooding world is undergoing climate change!" scientists warn. "Asteroids are headed our way!" the pundits cry, adding, "While we're streaming movies and taking selfies, terrorists are plotting, UFOs are hovering, and robots are quietly taking over. Everybody's colluding. And anybody saying anything different is spreading fake news."

You keep scrolling and clicking links. Global poverty, substance abuse, and health care costs are increasing even as safe food, clean water, and basic civility are disappearing. While you surf through a digital ocean of hopelessness, you're constantly reminded that viruses are mutating and pandemics are looming. *Click.* Unspeakable crime. *Click.* Unthinkable racism. *Click.* Heartbreaking despair.

You push away from the computer, sigh heavily, and feel doom and gloom descend on you like a thick mist. The world is unraveling!

What chance do we have? Perhaps you curl up in the fetal position. Or maybe you trudge to the freezer to comfort yourself with that pint of Ben & Jerry's ice cream—Blue Bell if you're a Texan.

Maybe, however, you don't need a bowl of Chocolate Fudge Brownie. Maybe all you really need is *a good spoiler.*

Spoilers are the worst! In the break room at work, you mention that you recorded the season finale of your favorite detective series so you can watch it over the weekend. Your inconsiderate coworker shakes his head and mumbles, "Yeah, I don't know how they're going to keep the show going without Captain Witmer! Crazy! That drug dealer guy *strangled* him!" (Suddenly, you're thinking of someone else who could use a little strangling.)

On the other hand, some people *love* spoilers. I learned this recently when I conducted a comprehensive and highly scientific poll[1] via Twitter and Facebook. I asked this question: "When reading a novel—especially a tense mystery or suspense thriller—do you ever skip ahead to the last chapter or page to find out how the book ends and calm your jangled nerves?"

Out of 93 respondents, a whopping 34 percent confessed to looking ahead! Of those who admitted peeking, some made comments like "If [the tension] is too much, I *have* to know the ending so I can calm down enough to read it." One confessed peeker wrote that a friend once told her about "a study that said people who know the endings ahead of time enjoy the journey more. So I'm going with that, LOL."

Believe it or not, such a study exists. It was conducted by Jonathan Leavitt and Nicholas Christenfeld of the University of California San Diego and reported in 2011 in the journal *Psychological Science*.[2] In three separate experiments, the professors discovered that rather than ruining one's "story experience," so-called "spoilers" enhance the enjoyment. Christenfeld likened this phenomenon to driving along a beautiful but perilous coastal highway. The first time you make the trip, you're a tightly wound knot of jittery nerves and white knuckles. You're so nervous about the road's twists and hairpin turns that you miss all the gorgeous scenery. But if you've made the trip before—and you know where the road leads—you can relax a bit and appreciate more of the beauty along the way.

This explains why we often enjoy films and books *more* the second or even third time around. It's why I often get sucked into certain movies—*The Fugitive, Apollo 13,* and *A Few Good Men,* for example—every time I come across them on TV and even though I practically have the endings memorized.

It seems two seemingly contradictory things are true at once: Some surprise is fun and welcome. Also, a little foreknowledge is a plus, not a minus.

The hack we need when we're reeling from all the woeful events unfolding around us? A simple, old-fashioned spoiler—reading or rereading Revelation 21 and 22, the last two chapters of the Bible. By looking ahead at what *will be*, we can find the hope we need to face what *is*.

At the end of Scripture, the apostle John glimpses both the end of the world as we know it and the beginning of the world to come. Limited by the inadequate language of earth, he struggles mightily to describe the ineffable realties of eternity.

He sees "a new heaven and a new earth." Then, suddenly, a city—identified by John as "the new Jerusalem"—comes down from heaven like a beautiful bride walking down the center aisle, all sparkly and shiny. Amid all this glory, John hears a loud announcement. The Lord God Almighty is present! Not to make a brief cameo appearance but to make himself at home! He's come to be with his people for good, to wipe away their tears and light up their lives forever. God declares an end to all the chaos and evil that has gripped the world since the great rebellion in paradise. "No more death or mourning or crying or pain" sounds very much like a return to Eden, doesn't it?

In down-to-earth terms, God's breathtaking promise here means no more dementia or burial plots, no more police blotters or courtrooms. To hear John tell it, the day will come when the world will have no need for oncologists or marriage counselors. We'll see an end—thank God Almighty—to racism, drug rehab facilities, orphanages, and sex trafficking.

Behind John's awe-filled descriptions, I can almost hear him whispering the same question Sam Gamgee poses at the end of J.R.R. Tolkien's *The Lord of the Rings*: "Is everything sad going to come untrue? What's happened to the world?"

God's answer—or at least his glad announcement? "I am making everything new!" (Revelation 21:5).

In a broken world where fallen people keep making foolish choices, John's vision is a good tonic and a helpful hack. It's a spoiler, all right—mostly spoiling all those gloomy, hopeless thoughts that continually try to lodge in our hearts.

# 35

# WHEN YOU KEEP FORGETTING WHAT MATTERS

One of the most haunting stories I know is told in Gabriel Garcia Márquez's acclaimed novel *One Hundred Years of Solitude*.

A strange plague sweeps through the remote Mexican town of Macondo, leaving all its residents with insomnia. But sleeplessness is not the worst of it. Soon the exhausted townspeople begin to slip into "the quicksand of forgetfulness." They can't recall the names of even simple, everyday items: a table, a chair, the clock, or the door. In a desperate attempt to jog their memories, they attach little labels to *everything*.

The image from this story that pierces my soul most? On the sign coming into town, they write the words "God exists."

My mother passed away in 2016 as a result of frontotemporal dementia. Someone described this terrible disease, which mimics

Alzheimer's, like this: Picture your brain as a giant erasable marker board filled with all the facts of your life. Each day the disease takes an eraser and makes another giant sweep across the board.

That's about right. Like the fictional residents of Macondo, Mom began forgetting common words: spoon, bowl, wheelchair. As time went on, she couldn't remember much of anything: how to put on a shoe, the names of her children, the fact that she'd been married for 66 of her 89 years.

If the ability to remember is an astonishing blessing, the fact of forgetfulness is a terrible curse.

It seems to me that we remember in two basic ways. The first works something like this: You're going about your life, and unexpectedly—because of a voice maybe, or an old song or a certain smell—you're transported from the present into the past. Suddenly, in your mind's eye, you're seeing a long-forgotten face or reliving an experience you hadn't thought of in ages. This kind of remembering can be either sweet or bitter. Often, it's a little bit of both.

A second kind of remembering is intentional, not accidental. Instead of passively waiting for random memories to surface, we *try* to recall important events, facts, or experiences. We practice this kind of remembering when we put birthday reminders and appointment alerts in our smartphones and when we slip wedding bands on our fingers. We do it when we memorize—that is, commit to memory—inspiring words so we can repeat them to ourselves in discouraging moments. We do it when we set aside special days for somber reflection (like Good Friday and Memorial Day). Unlike reactive remembering, this more proactive version of remembering isn't interested in nostalgic excursions back in time. On the contrary, it seeks out meaningful events, promises, or lessons from the past and exports them into the present.

Care to guess which kind of remembering will do the most good for your soul?

The Israelites were antsy to enter the promised land. Their leader, Moses, was hesitant to let them go, a lot like a nervous parent dropping off a firstborn child at college. When Moses realized he wasn't long for this world, this man who once insisted his skill set didn't include public speaking (Exodus 4:10) launched into a kind of spiritual filibuster. Suddenly, he was a fountain of lectures, final instructions, and last-minute warnings.

In his last words—i.e., the book of Deuteronomy—Moses spoke extensively about the human tendency to forget *spiritual* truth and the urgent need to remember it.[1] The gist of his message? *Don't forget that God exists!* The Hebrew word translated "remember" is *zakar* and—surprise!—it's a reference to that second form of remembering, the active, purposeful variety. It means "to recall or bring to mind." Moses was pleading with the Jewish people to be intentional—to make vigorous and regular efforts to summon up the truths and lessons from the past that would make life better for them in the present.

For example, Moses urged the Israelites to remember the miraculous way God had delivered them from Egypt (Deuteronomy 5:15; 16:3). He exhorted them to call to mind the dramatic encounter they had with God at Mount Sinai (Deuteronomy 4:10-12). In another place, he said, "Remember how the Lord your God led you all the way in the wilderness these forty years" (Deuteronomy 8:2). Translation: "Recall God's faithfulness and guidance and patience with you when you were being your most stubborn, petulant selves."

Before he was finished, Moses even urged the people to remember their most forgettable moment as a people (Deuteronomy 9:7)—when they impulsively made a golden idol and bowed to it shortly after pledging wholehearted devotion to God. Calling this grievous sin to mind would be important, not for the purpose of wallowing in guilt but so they could maintain a healthy fear of what the human heart is capable of when it forgets God.

In effect, Moses was saying, "Each time you purposely recall any of these experiences, it'll be like looking at a 'God exists' sign."

What do you know? Almost three and a half millennia ago, Moses was hinting at the scientific truths now being discovered by twenty-first-century neurologists. One of their current theories about memory is that whenever we acquire new information we deem important, our brains a) store that fact or experience and b) create a pathway—or memory trace—to where that image or information is stored. The theory argues that the more often we access that stored information, the more easily we can find and use it in the future.

However, if over time we don't use the mental pathways designed to help us retrieve certain bits of information, those memory traces become harder and harder to distinguish—almost like hiking trails in the forest that go unused and eventually become overgrown and lost. The desired information might still be there in our long-term memory, but we won't be able to retrieve it easily, and it will be of no use to us.

Sobered by the realities of dementia and Alzheimer's, more and more people are scrambling to stave off memory loss. I have friends who are modifying their diets, and my wife is wolfing down walnuts because they are supposedly good for brain health. Others are increasing social interactions, becoming more active physically, and seeking mental stimulation through activities such as reading, working crossword puzzles, playing bridge, and doing puzzles.

What about our tendency to forget *spiritual* truth? Can we fight this "dementia of the soul" in practical ways? Absolutely. Via all sorts of hacks and intentional acts, we can erect little "God exists" signs in our lives.

- *Reading and rereading the story of God and his people.* I have friends who make it a priority to read the entire Bible in a year, every year. It sounds intimidating, but it's honestly not hard to do. All it takes is reading three chapters a day (five on Sundays).

- *Writing a brief account of how God opened your eyes to the truth of the gospel.* Simply describe the circumstances that prompted you to put your faith in Christ. Then tell that story to others and encourage them to tell you their own unique stories. Reviewing our own salvation stories and hearing how God has called other people to himself serve as powerful reminders that God is—and that he is active in the world.

- *Committing to memory one new Bible verse a week, and then reviewing it daily for a week, weekly for a month, and monthly for a year.* Imagine that. At the end of one year, you could have more than 50 verses stored in your mind and heart! In ten years, you could have more than 500 memorized verses tucked away!

- *Participating fully in Christian community.* By gathering regularly with other believers to pray, study Scripture, worship, and serve together, you receive regular reminders of the reality of God, his love, and his power.

- *Creating a written record of key moments in our lives when God's presence and power were undeniably real.* Pull out this record, add to it over time, and review it when your faith is flagging.

- *Starting a prayer journal where we keep a record of answered prayers.* Nothing shouts, "God exists!" more than rereading how he healed a friendship, invaded a heart, restored a marriage, or said no to one stubborn request so that eventually he could give something far better.

- *Building a memorial to God's faithfulness.* Memorials can be almost anything: stones (see chapter 33), framed letters, or snapshots of big events. Maybe your memorial could be a wall of pictures—all the people who have pointed you to God. Maybe it could be a shelf of the books God has used most to ignite and strengthen your faith.

My mother, bless her heart, fought a valiant fight against dementia. By her final year it had erased almost every memory she had. But not all of them. For the longest time she could still hum along to the old hymns she'd learned as a child. And in disturbing, confusing moments—and there were many of those—her first instinct was always to pray. Up until her last three or four months, she remembered to do one thing every morning—reach for the old King James Bible sitting next to her old La-Z-Boy recliner.

In my mind's eye, I can see her still, holding that precious book close to her eyes, her own personal "God exists" sign.

# 36

# WHEN YOU'RE WONDERING, HOW LONG WILL I NEED TO KEEP HACKING MY HEART?

An unbreakable law is at work in life, and we can state it this way: *Everything slowly becomes shabby.*

This rule is like gravity; it has no exceptions. In a fallen world, decline into disorder *is* the natural order. The evidence is everywhere we turn: the cracking pavement, the peeling paint, the receding hairline, the wrinkled skin, the truck that needs new brakes, the flower bed that needs constant weeding.

*Entropy* is the term some people use to describe this relentless dissolution. And it affects more than just physical objects. Entropy is what's happening when a smartly run business becomes sloppy, when a powerful movement runs out of steam, when a marriage crumbles, when a heart grows cold.

At the end of his life, when Moses was bidding farewell to his fellow Israelites, do you know what concerned him most? Entropy. Or more precisely, the very real danger of *spiritual* entropy. This would explain why he pleaded, "Be careful, and watch yourselves closely so that you do not forget the things your eyes have seen or let them fade from your heart as long as you live" (Deuteronomy 4:9).

If that ancient warning doesn't take away your breath, you might want to check to see if you have any breath left for the taking. Moses was saying, "The moment you stop watching over your heart, entropy begins doing its destructive work." If we aren't vigilant, all those life-altering things we saw God do or heard him say yesterday and today will be lost to us tomorrow. Those truths will fade from our hearts. We will become shabby…slowly, steadily, certainly.

"Okay, okay. I get it," we say. "Hacking my heart is important. Just tell me how long I need to keep at it." Moses's commands to "be careful" and "watch yourselves closely" tell us how long—for the rest of our earthly lives!

Here again we see a fundamental difference between *life hacks* and *spiritual life hacks*. Most life hacks are creative fixes or slick work-arounds we need only occasionally (like using Doritos to start a campfire).

The best spiritual life hacks are habitual acts. They make a difference in our lives because we practice them regularly. (That's the ironic truth about having good habits: If you stop doing them for a week or two, you no longer have them!)

What are we saying here? That spiritual entropy is real, that it will attack even our good habits, and therefore, we can never stop hacking. Slack off, and the truths that matter most will soon start slipping from our souls.

One warm afternoon many springs ago, I took my wife on a grand tour of the grounds of our palatial estate—all .34 acres of it. Playing the role of pseudo-horticulturist, I pointed out all the reasons we wouldn't be winning Yard of the Month. I gestured toward our sickly rose garden, a bed of azaleas infested with lace bugs, and a gardenia bush that looked, frankly, as if it had just been cursed by Jesus. I noted with dismay the chickweed, dandelions, and wild onions flourishing inside the same circular brown patches where our centipede grass was being ravaged by some kind of killer fungus. (Bunny Trail Question: Why can't scientists get the pests to eat the weeds instead of the good plants and then have the fungi kill only the pests?)

My saintly wife listened to my garden-grumbling for several minutes. Then she smiled sweetly and said softly, "You want heaven."

Only three words, but an ocean of insight. I don't merely want a weed-free lawn; I want a flaw-free world.

I'm not alone in this desire. You want the same thing: children who never hurt or make bad choices, relationships void of all dysfunction, work so satisfying it doesn't feel like work, a body that never aches or tires, a mind that can *always* recall names and retrieve facts.

*Of course* we want heaven! As the offspring of Adam and Eve, we carry faint memories of Eden within our souls. Why else would beauty pierce our hearts the way it does? We're homesick for the paradise we lost. Because we can't go back, we can only gawk longingly at the stunning picture painted in Revelation 21–22.

And while we wait? We hack! It's in our nature. We instinctively know that all things and all people are meant to be better than they are. So, whenever we notice a broken thing that needs fixing or a good thing that could be tweaked into something better, we can't help ourselves. Off we go, tenaciously tinkering, nervously noodling. Wanting heaven is why we rebuild the engine and rework the recipe. It's why we rethink the process. Reorganize the closet. Resume the diet. Renew our marriage vows. Write the book.

The truth? We want heaven. The good news? One day we will have it. And not just heaven, but a "new heaven"—and a new earth to boot! (Revelation 21:1).

What will the life to come be like? The Bible doesn't give us many specifics, only this big overview: We, the people of God, with redeemed souls, renewed minds, and restored bodies, will one day live face-to-face with the One in whose image we are made.

In his devotional masterpiece *Diary of an Old Soul*, George Mac-Donald speculated prayerfully—and excitedly—about what we might *do* in eternity:

> What if thou make us able to make like thee—
> To light with moons, to clothe with greenery,
> To hang gold sunsets o'er a rose and purple sea![1]

It's a heart-stopping thought; it also happens to make a lot of logical and theological sense. We are made in the image of the Ultimate Maker, and we are being conformed to the image of Christ. Doesn't it follow that in the future, Revelation 23 and beyond, we "chips off the eternal block" would be makers too?

Imagine getting to use all our purified, glorified, hacking ingenuity in a brand-new world with no problems, just limitless potential. With the fall and all its frustrations in our rearview mirror, there'll be no fixing what's broken, only exploring what's possible. We'll have the ultimate workshop/laboratory/playground/stage/canvas for all our God-given creativity!

The promise of the gospel sounds too good to be true. But it *is* true. God has reconciled us to himself through Christ. He's ushered us into a new life that will never end. That's more than a guaranteed future; it's hope *now*. The Holy One has moved into our lives and is in the process of transforming us today—from the inside out.

With holy courage and sanctified inventiveness, then, the task before us is clear. We're to keep finding innovative ways to wake and turn and open our hearts to the One who made them. By his sweet grace and in his limitless strength, we will hack our way home.

# LIST OF SPIRITUAL LIFE HACKS

1. When you're wondering where to start hacking...**start with your heart.**

2. When you feel disillusioned by your lack of spiritual growth...**stop waiting for a holy "zap" and start working out.**

3. When you're heading out into a problem-filled world...**stick a few "Hosannas!" in your pocket.**

4. When you can't see God working in your life...**see (with eyes of faith) beyond your little knothole.**

5. When you're battling doubts...**review your ABCs.**

6. When you feel overwhelmed...**make a good list and check it twice.**

7. When life is full of uncertainty...**relax! He knows...you know?**

8. When you're knackered...**consider what the Lord promises knackered souls.**

9. When it's taking a long time to bounce back from a draining experience…**surrender to God's timetable.**

10. When the idea of repenting leaves you cold…**repent of your bogus ideas about repentance.**

11. When you need to pray but you're all out of words…**try a "breath prayer."**

12. When your devotional life is stale and blah…**throw it a curveball.**

13. When you're feeling big pressure to rescue someone… **stick to the role God's assigned you in his big Story.**

14. When your faith is overdue for a checkup…**face up to the intrusive questions of Jesus.**

15. When your heart is full (but not in the best of ways or with the best of things)…**dump the junk and get a refill.**

16. When you're too wrapped up in your own life…**go grab a cup of joe with Joe (or Jo).**

17. When you're not in a great place (emotionally speaking)…**find somebody to love.**

18. When you're tired of all the pretending…**grab your soul by the collar and tell it the hard truth about being truthful.**

19. When you're not sure what to say…**say what you *need* to say.**

20. When you could stand to be more thankful…**consider the upside of being a "Grateful."**

21. When you're forced to be around somebody really annoying…**practice a different kind of TLC**

22. When your soul is all stirred up…**find a peaceful spot and still your heart.**

23. When you get an encouraging note…**stick it in your Barnabas box.**

24. When you're disgusted with yourself because of all the things you "should" be doing but aren't…**listen to the one voice that matters.**

25. When you're irritated by all those pesky people in your way…**engage in a little guerrilla praying.**

26. When you're ready to quit…**show up *one more time*.**

27. When you've decided you have nothing to offer anyone…**stop comparing, assess your uniqueness, and join the party!**

28. When you find yourself a little too concerned about "him," "her," or "them"…**take a break from social media and police your own life.**

29. When you don't feel like doing what you need to do…**put your feelings in their place "by faith."**

30. When you're in a Psalm 98 worship service with a Psalm 88 heart…**remember that crying can be as good for the soul as clapping.**

31. When productivity starts to become a problem…**take a break—less really *can* be more.**

32. When you're starting something…**start with this (personal) presentation.**

33. When things in your life are shaky...**grab a rock.**

34. When everything seems doomy and gloomy...**peek ahead at the ultimate spoiler.**

35. When you keep forgetting what matters...**erect some "God exists!" signs.**

36. When you're wondering, *How long will I need to keep hacking my heart?...* **resist the law of entropy and keep hacking toward home.**

# NOTES

## WHAT THE HECK IS A "HACK"?

1. Merriam-Webster.com, https://www.merriam-webster.com/dictionary/hack#h1.

2. The CBS series *MacGyver* that began airing in 2016 is a reboot of the original.

3. Leon Ho, "Welcome to Lifehack!" email newsletter sent to new subscribers (2/9/19).

4. Ibid.

5. I never heard that old preacher enumerate the Bible's big ideas, but I'd state them this way: 1. God exists. 2. God is worth knowing, loving, and serving. 3. Humans tend to resent, rebel against, and run from God. 4. God sent Jesus Christ to seek and save us. 5. We're called to live by faith. 6. There's more to life than just this life. 7. God designed us to live in healthy relationship with others. 8. Ultimately, all will be well.

## CHAPTER 1: WHEN YOU'RE WONDERING WHERE TO START HACKING

1. This is how we know a subject is a big deal to God: It comes up again and again in Scripture.

## CHAPTER 2: WHEN YOU FEEL DISILLUSIONED BY YOUR LACK OF SPIRITUAL GROWTH

1. Flannery O'Connor, *Mystery and Manners: Occasional Prose* (New York: Farrar, Straus and Giroux, 1969), 44.

2. How does one manage to tithe 2.5 cents a week? Easy. You alternate—two cents one week, three the next. The power of math!

3. While writing this chapter, I had lunch with a long-time friend whose wife found dramatic freedom from the eating disorder bulimia nervosa while a college student. One day, after many people had been praying for her for a long time, her overpowering compulsion to binge-eat and then purge was simply gone. She was free. I've known other Christian women who experienced victory over bulimia—but *eventually*, only after a long, hard, spiritual struggle.

## CHAPTER 3: WHEN YOU'RE HEADING OUT INTO A PROBLEM-FILLED WORLD

1. Duct tape was originally known as "duck tape" because of its cloth/scrim waterproof backing. Duck Tape is now a well-known brand of duct tape.

2. Some people swear that duct-taping a wart for six days will kill it.

3. Thanks in large part to duct tape, the Apollo 13 crew made it back to earth in a badly damaged spacecraft.

4. God knows the exact moment this miracle—being declared as righteous and passing from death to life—happened for us even if we don't.

## CHAPTER 4: WHEN YOU CAN'T SEE GOD WORKING IN YOUR LIFE

1. Exodus, the second book of the Bible, begins with the children of Jacob living like royalty in Egypt, experiencing a baby boom, and growing into 12 large tribes. As a result—major plot twist—Egypt's new ruler decides to make slaves out of these "resident aliens." They remain in bondage for *centuries*.

2. The Israelites' desperation is heard in the Hebrew verb translated "cried out." This is the same word used in 2 Samuel 13 to describe the reaction of a rape victim. It's used in 2 Samuel 19 to describe David's reaction when he got the news that his son had been killed. When you do the math (compare Exodus 2:11-22 with Acts 7:30), you realize that such agonized praying went on for *40 years*!

3. I've heard several people—most recently John Piper—express variations of this idea that we probably see only two or three of God's orchestrations at a time.

4. DreamWorks is the studio cofounded by Stephen Spielberg and famous for making *The Prince of Egypt*—an animated movie about the life of *Moses*! Irony? Or God's funny little sense of humor?

## CHAPTER 5: WHEN YOU'RE BATTLING DOUBTS

1. My guess is that Annie's friends went immediately to DEFCON 1 in their reaction because she was putting words to some of the same disturbing questions swirling in their own hearts—troubling thoughts they were too afraid to face. I have a strong feeling that if you gave them all shots of Sodium Pentothal (aka truth serum), they'd admit as much. It's human nature to save one's fiercest denunciations for the problems that hit closest to home.

## CHAPTER 6: WHEN YOU FEEL OVERWHELMED

1. David Wallechinsky, Amy D. Wallace, Ira Basen, and Jane Farrow, *The Book of Lists* (Knopf Canada, 2012), x.

## CHAPTER 7: WHEN LIFE IS FULL OF UNCERTAINTY

1. This prediction was originally mentioned in a paper ("The Toxic Terabyte: How Data Dumping Threatens Business Efficiency") published by IBM Global Technology Services in July 2006. See http://www-935.ibm.com/services/no/cio/leverage/levinfo_wp_gts_thetoxic.pdf. It was reported by David Russell Schilling, "Knowledge Doubling Every 12 Months, Soon to Be Every 12 Hours" in Industry Tap into News, April 19, 2013, http://www.industrytap.com/knowledge-doubling -every-12-months-soon-to-be-every-12-hours/3950.

2. I can report that our old Amana finally gave up the ghost during the editing of this book, meaning my family likely witnessed the longest, slowest death in major appliance history.

3. See 2 Samuel 7:20; 1 Kings 8:39; 1 Chronicles 17:18; 2 Chronicles 6:30; Psalm 40:9; 69:19; 139:2, 4; Jeremiah 12:3; Ezekiel 37:3; John 16:30; 21:15-17.

4. Matthew 26:69-75; Mark 14:66-72; Luke 22:54-62; John 18:15-18,25-27.

## CHAPTER 10: WHEN THE IDEA OF REPENTING LEAVES YOU COLD

1. My friend Dave calls this strange practice of preaching to others by spray painting words on overpasses "evandalism."

2. The word *repent* often has three syllables in the Deep South (and sometimes four if the preacher is on a roll).

## CHAPTER 11: WHEN YOU NEED TO PRAY BUT YOU'RE ALL OUT OF WORDS

1. The "Jesus Prayer" is adapted from Luke 18:13 and 39.

2. A fascinating book called *The Way of the Pilgrim*, published in the late nineteenth century, documents one Russian Christian's attempt to "pray continually."

## CHAPTER 12: WHEN YOUR DEVOTIONAL LIFE IS STALE AND BLAH

1. C.S. Lewis, *The Screwtape Letters* (New York, NY: HarperCollins, 2001), 40.

## CHAPTER 13: WHEN YOU'RE FEELING BIG PRESSURE TO RESCUE SOMEONE

1. The fact that Donnie Bryant's asking me to meet him in the lobby of a fancy hotel didn't cause alarm bells to go off in my head is proof of either what a great con man he was or what a sucker I was—or both.

2. If you checked this box about letting a con man guilt you into giving him $300, give me a shout and let's compare notes and commiserate together.

## CHAPTER 14: WHEN YOUR FAITH IS OVERDUE FOR A CHECKUP

1. When a doctor or doctor's nurse says, "How about we step up on the scales here and get our weight?" I always want to reply, "Trust me. The number will be plenty big enough if we just get *my* weight."

2. I am a big believer in flossing. "Be true to your teeth," I like to say, "and they'll never be false to you."

3. In his book *Jesus Is the Question*, Martin Copenhaver lists 307 questions asked by Jesus in the Gospels.

## CHAPTER 15: WHEN YOUR HEART IS FULL (BUT NOT IN THE BEST OF WAYS OR WITH THE BEST OF THINGS)

1. I cup my hands while praying in private, usually before the world wakes up, not in public with the world watching. That would look pretty weird.

## CHAPTER 16: WHEN YOU'RE TOO WRAPPED UP IN YOUR OWN LIFE

1. I could tell you exactly where my SelfIshNess card is, except I was terrible at keeping Teen Commandment #5, "Take care of your possessions."

## CHAPTER 18: WHEN YOU'RE TIRED OF ALL THE PRETENDING

1. C.S. Lewis, *Letters to Malcolm: Chiefly on Prayer* (New York, NY: HarperCollins, 1992), 27.

2. In Acts 1:24, the apostles refer to God as *kardiognostes*, literally "the one who knows the heart." This descriptive title for God is derived from two Greek words, *kardia*, or heart, and *gnosis*, or knowledge.

## CHAPTER 19: WHEN YOU'RE NOT SURE WHAT TO SAY

1. This figure is based on two sets of data: 1) research conducted by Dr. James Pennebaker and others in the psychology department at the University of Texas (and reported in the journal *Science* in 2007), which found that female subjects spoke, on average, 16,215 words a day and male participants, 15,669 words daily. (It should be noted that some test subjects spoke as few as 500 words a day; others as many as 47,000!); 2) current CDC life expectancy rates for Americans (78.8 as of 2017).

2. We are replacing our hips and knees left and right, when the average number of steps taken by an average, moderately active person—143,810,000 in a lifetime (5,000 per day x 78.8 years)—is *less* than one third the number of words we say. See Wendy Bumgardner, "How Many Average Daily Steps People Walk," verywellfit.com, October 1, 2018, https://www.verywellfit.com/whats-typical-for-average-daily-steps-3435736.

3. Conversations to iron out differences should *never* happen on social media or even via email. Face-to-face is what you want. If geography is a problem, the phone can suffice, but make the call using video technology.

4. The Greek word literally means "rotten." Other modern Bible translations render this word in English as "corrupting talk" (esv) or "foul or abusive language" (nlt).

## CHAPTER 20: WHEN YOU COULD STAND TO BE MORE THANKFUL

1. I heard Ms. Gilbert tell this story in an interview with Krista Tippett on the "On Being" podcast that aired July 7, 2016.

## CHAPTER 22: WHEN YOUR SOUL IS ALL STIRRED UP

1. A ficus tree in Bihar, India, under which Siddhartha Gautama (aka the Buddha) is said to have attained enlightenment.

2. In truth, the entire world is holy, because there's no place where God is not. Some places only *seem* holier because we're not paying close attention in the other places.

3. This is one of the fascinating things about Rocky Mountain National Park—the weather changes constantly. The joke among locals is, "Here you can sometimes experience all four seasons in a single day." I don't know about that, but I do recall sweating heavily while hiking once in late May—and then getting snowed on in the same day.

## CHAPTER 26: WHEN YOU'RE READY TO QUIT

1. Currently, my most precious assets are a collection of old presidential campaign buttons and a six-year-old MacBook Pro.

2. Choe Sang-Hun, "At First She Didn't Succeed, but She Tried and Tried Again (960 Times)," *The New York Times*, September 3, 2010, https://www.nytimes.com/2010/09/04/world/asia/04driver.html.

## CHAPTER 28: WHEN YOU FIND YOURSELF A LITTLE TOO CONCERNED ABOUT "HIM," "HER," OR "THEM"

1. These two disciples—Peter and John—seem to have had a competitive relationship (see John 20:3-4).

## CHAPTER 29: WHEN YOU DON'T FEEL LIKE DOING WHAT YOU NEED TO DO

1. This statement is about living by faith (coming to know God by faith and then walking with God in continuing trust). It's so fundamental that it's repeated three times in the New Testament (Romans 1:17; Galatians 3:11; Hebrews 10:38).

2. C.S. Lewis, *The World's Last Night and Other Essays* (New York, NY: Harcourt, Brace and Company, 1952), 109.

## CHAPTER 30: WHEN YOU'RE IN A PSALM 98 WORSHIP SERVICE WITH A PSALM 88 HEART

1. It's doubtful that worship pastors, as a group, heed any verse in the Bible more than Psalm 98:1.